Understanding Illustration

Derek Brazell and **Jo Davies**

First published in Great Britain in 2014
Bloomsbury Visual Arts, an imprint of
Bloomsbury Publishing Plc
50 Bedford Square
London W1CB 3DP

1385 Broadway
New York
NY 10018
USA

www.bloomsbury.com

Bloomsbury is a registered trademark of
Bloomsbury Publishing Plc

ISBN 978-1-408-17179-0

Copyright © Derek Brazell & Jo Davies 2014

CIP Catalogue records for this book are
available from the British Library.

Book design by Simon Sharville.
www.simonsharville.co.uk

Cover design by Eleanor Rose.
Cover illustration by Lesley Barnes.

Printed and bound in China.

Acknowledgements

We're continuously impressed with the generosity of illustrators,
and we'd like to sincerely thank all the artists who gave their time
to discuss their projects with us for *Understanding Illustration*, as
well as allowing their amazing artwork to be featured.

Thanks to our editor at Bloomsbury, Alison Stace, and all our
family and friends for their support over the time it has taken to
complete the book.
Plymouth University's generous support freed time for Jo to
undertake research.
All the publishers and companies whose commissions are
published here, including:
Adobe, Balzer + Bray, Channel 4 Television and VideoText
Communications Ltd, Picturehouse Television Co. Ltd, Wildfire
TV, The Folio Society, Ghosts of Gone Birds, The Guardian,
Meathaus SOS, National Post, Nelson Beer, Penguin USA,
Phaidon, Puffin Books, Rough Trade Records, Schwartz &
Wade, Sunday New York Times, Templar Publishing, The
Washington Spectator, Wilkins Farago, Walker Books, UNESCO,
US Postal Service, Varoom/Association of Illustrators.

Images reproduced on pages 27 and 29 from *The Onion's Great
Escape*, published by Phaidon Press Limited. Copyright © 2012
Sara Fanelli and Phaidon Press Limited.

Jo Davies and Derek Brazell

Contents

Introduction

Understanding Illustration examines an eclectic and carefully selected set of images and projects that consider the function of illustrative imagery and the context in which it is created, including the breadth of subjects illustration deals with and the processes and interactions involved in its creation and interpretation.

The term 'illustration' increasingly embraces an intriguing diversity of practices and outcomes, and this book offers a greater understanding of the subject through first-hand interviews and the insights of 36 artists.

Many perspectives can be drawn upon in attempting to understand illustration, including philosophical, aesthetic and cultural outlooks. The range of interpretation is a reminder that encounters with this subject can be engaging and also challenging.

What is certain is that when an image is viewed outside the context that it is designed for, providing evidence of its function, intention, message and culture, the reading and evaluation of a piece of illustration is limited and its value potentially diminished. Examining the fabric of an illustration requires some understanding of the brief, why an illustration was commissioned, the motivation behind its creation. Such investigation is needed if appraisal of an image is to stretch beyond a merely superficial judgement of its immediate aesthetic and surface properties.

Historically, technology has impacted upon the forms and extent of distribution of illustrated works, as well as the engineering of images. Increasingly, this has led to an extension of illustration beyond the printed surface to occupy multi-dimensional spaces. Illustrators are communicating through an expanding repertoire of forms, screen-based and moving imagery, toys, site-specific work and installations, as well as traditional print-based formats. The largely unrevealed material factors, processes and intentions leading to a work's generation can provide vital clues towards a fuller understanding of contemporary practice.

Illustration is an important global economic force providing employment for a significant number of people. Financial transactions underpin its creation, application and distribution. An image can be instrumental in selling a product, service or idea. In the USA the change in the nomenclature of the profession in the 1950s, relabelling illustration as commercial art, reflected a shift in the functional relationship of imagery to traditional narrative and literary contexts towards a role focused on selling.

The function of illustration in the 21st century continues to be influenced by economic forces, spearheaded by the requirements of clients who bring a multiplicity of influential factors to the creative process – including the practical constraints of budget, time and dimensions. These collaborations between designers, illustrators and creators of content are intertwining threads of involvement, often embedded in the work but concealed by the final form of the illustrative artefact. Authorial projects may reveal a more direct visual voice, often unencumbered by commercial considerations, although these can also develop into marketable ventures.

Through direct reference to political and social issues in history, illustration has proven that it holds power culturally, influencing social mores, public opinion and behaviour. It is also instrumental educationally, ratifying and illuminating across platforms and reaching audiences of all ages and demographics. Whether included with, or independent of, text-based environments, an image can provide clarity and promote understanding and learning. Illustration is also adept at entertaining and providing aesthetic sustenance through decoration. In each of these instances the messages and meanings are distinctive and the process of communication complex and unique.

In illustration the form often follows the function. The formats for which an artwork is created, such as the functional relationship an image asserts when combined with text in contributing to the narrative in a book, are different from an artwork's purpose and interpretation when applied as a decorative element on the surface of an object, or adding to the pathways through an interactive website.

Whether representational, schematic, using symbols or lyrical expression, illustrators' styles embody distinctive visual codes specific to their culture. Employing the pictorial conventions of composition, line, texture, colour and form fundamental to creative activity, illustrators create personal artistic languages that communicate effectively and are often used for visual problem-solving. The involvement of the viewer can also bring intentional or additional meanings to the work.

The look of an era can be defined by the prevalent visual trends emerging from both the mainstream and personal practice of its prominent practitioners. Illustration is at once a social signifier and a social force – a measure of the osmosis of commercial art into popular culture and the pervasive force of imagery within subcultures such as graffiti and urban art.

Each image included in *Understanding Illustration* reveals something about the subject in the 21st century, whether about the power of illustration, the subjects it deals with, the way that illustration functions, the way that artists work or the relationships that underpin the artwork.

Interviews with the featured illustrators allowed for the identification of the various forces and motives influencing the creator at the time of working on a specific piece and the factors underpinning their output in general. Cumulatively, through classifying and examining the context for which the work was produced, a greater understanding is provided of the meaning of a focused selection representing the best of practice.

By presenting images within such a broad framework, this collection emphasises the value of each piece, revealing layers of meaning within the fascinating subject of contemporary illustration.

Narrative – The Book
Narrative – Children's Books
Traditional Contexts

01 Traditional Uses

Images have been an intrinsic element of printed communication for centuries, and as applications for illustration continue to expand, the traditional areas of advertising, design and publishing continue to utilise the strength of imagery.

The book cover remains a strong selling point for publishing, especially for adult and children's fiction, attracting the attention of readers whether on digital store 'bookshelves', webpages of online retailers or the physical ones of bookstores. The cover illustration presents a narrative that helps create an identity for an author as well as drawing in potential readers.

The design of some covers has continued to incorporate hand-rendered typography, as demonstrated by the *Jane Austen* covers by Audrey Niffenegger, (see pp.10–13), merging design and illustration into a unified whole. Within children's publishing the strength of illustration to transcend fashions and continue to appeal to successive generations is demonstrated by Jan Pieńkowski's work for folklore and fairy tales. The apparent simplicity of his silhouetted images remains ageless. Moreover, the ability of illustrated stories aimed at children to cover subjects of weight and importance remains strong. Kadir Nelson's *Heart and Soul* delivers an accessible history of the African American experience, allowing for empathy to develop between the subject and the reader.

The physical book has been a mainstay of the publishing world, but as once standard formats are superseded by new platforms, there are artists still developing the physical book beyond its typical structure, effectively differentiating it from the digital, and providing tangible evidence that the book as artefact will survive in some form. Artists like Sara Fanelli explore the boundaries of the format, producing challenging and entertaining structures. Her book *The Onion's Great Escape* gives young readers increased physical engagement with the physical object. The character of the Onion is separated page by page until it 'escapes' the book, while still retaining its shape.

In recent years the popularity of the graphic novel has become more widespread, at the same time winning critical approval as the format expands in inventiveness and subject matter. Artists around the world are adapting the form to explore new areas including making social comment and autobiographical investigation through layered storytelling. Asaf and Tomer Hanuka are key exponents of this genre. Their collaborative work for *The Dirties* uses personally inspired narratives and optimises digital platforms as a means to distribution.

The persuasive power of illustrated images runs through editorial, design and packaging, offering a multitude of options with which clients can impress their message on the intended audience. As with books, cover artwork for a magazine has a vital role to play in attracting the reader, and George Hardie's intriguing take on the spot-the-difference picture for *Varoom* magazine, for instance, shows that an image of some complexity can successfully work as a visual hook.

Since the 1950s photography has competed with illustration within the realm of advertising, but the industry continues to recognise the value in using illustration and is always looking for new approaches to reach its audience. Gail Armstrong brings an element of innovation through her use of paper sculpture, combining a three-dimensional perspective with a humorous, narrative-based concept.

As with advertising, packaging illustration is adept at ensuring that products stand out from their competitors, targeting potential customers with imagery to indicate freshness, authenticity or coolness to attract a certain demographic. Australian collective WeBuyYourKids show how personal interests can feed into highly commercial commissions. Their practice is another example of collaboration at its best.

Examining the work in this section reveals that 'traditional' does not necessarily equate with staid or predictable responses to briefs and that innovative and thoughtful practice prevails within commercial illustration.

Audrey Niffenegger
Jane Austen book covers

While known for her own novels and artist's books, including *Three Incestuous Sisters* and *The Nightmobile*, a commission from Penguin USA to illustrate Jane Austen's last published novel, *Persuasion*, was enthusiastically accepted by Audrey Niffenegger. *Persuasion* was part of a new Penguin Classics Deluxe Editions series, many of which were being illustrated by renowned comic artists, including Robert Crumb, Chris Ware and Art Spiegelman – prompting Audrey to comment that it was "a strange and illicit thrill to be in that kind of company". Her visual approach doesn't change when illustrating another writer's text. "My work always seems to end up looking like my work. The fact that the series is comics-based was influential." Penguin Art Director, Paul Buckley, had decided to challenge the general perceptions of readers by reinvigorating these classics, saying to her, "Take it out there!" Following successful delivery of the *Persuasion* cover, she was also asked to create the artwork for Austen's *Sense and Sensibility*.

Classic novel covers have a lineage which an artist might avoid, but as Audrey owns multiple editions of all Jane Austen's books, there was no getting away from other *Persuasion* covers, "The previous editions used 19th-century portraits of women, all very serious ladies. But I knew Paul wanted something different."

"The book you remember is never the book you reread," recalls Audrey of *Persuasion*, which was initially published posthumously in 1818. What impressed itself upon her this time around was how trapped the

Persuasion by Jane Austen,
Art Director Paul Buckley, published by Penguin Classics Deluxe Editions, 2011. Front cover (right) and wrap (left). Original artwork before colour adjustments for print.

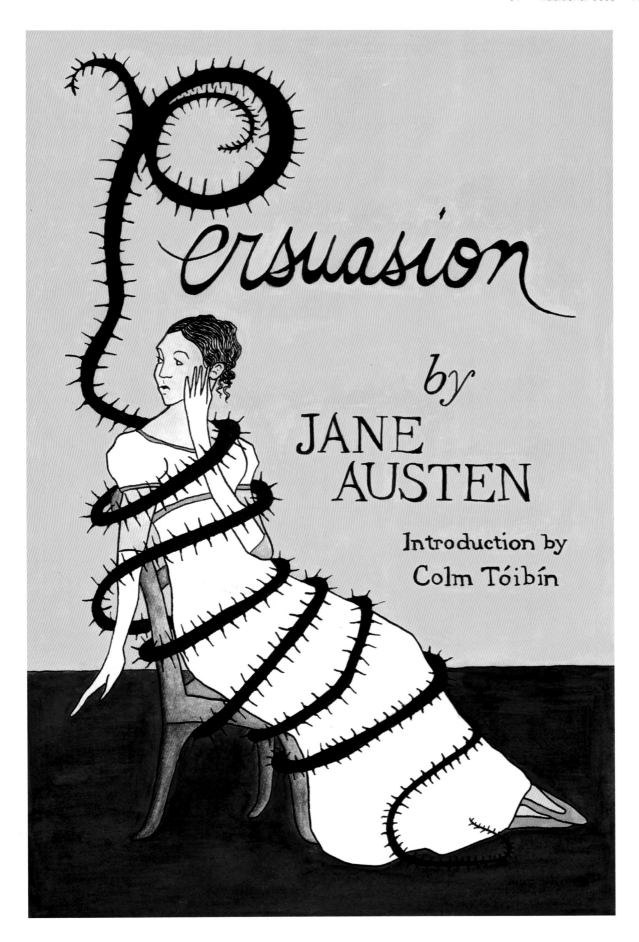

"I've got to abandon this notion of depicting these characters. How does this thing feel, really?"

She had an excellent heart;— her disposition was affectionate, and her feelings were strong; but she knew how to govern them: it was a knowledge which her mother had yet to learn, and which one of her sisters had resolved never to be taught.

Jane Austen SENSE and Sensibility

SENSE and Sensibility

Foreword by Cathleen Schine

by JANE AUSTEN

Bicentennial Edition

Cover Art by Audrey Niffenegger

Sense and Sensibility by Jane Austen, original artwork before colour adjustments for print. Art Director Paul Buckley, Penguin Classics Deluxe Editions series, 2011

main character of Anne Elliot was by her family and society's conventions. One of the consistent elements of the series was hand-rendered type, and her original concept became the binding title lettering. "That was the first idea I had when I re-read the text, that Anne was being bound by persuasion itself, that the very words all her people were saying to her were strangling her." This was further developed by the shape of the word being formed of a briar stem. "It does look much more unpleasant with thorns, doesn't it?" The cover texts, including credits and back-cover blurb, were all applied directly onto the artwork in one layer, by hand with a crow quill pen.

Both books' covers are wraparounds, allowing for continued extensions of the front cover concept. For *Persuasion*, the cover briars blossom into roses on the interior flaps. "I was thinking about the reputation of Jane Austen's work as 'romance'. When you read her actual work, she's not at all starry-eyed or frilly; she's very hard-edged about the realities of marriage and money and what it takes to make society function. So the roses are meant to reference romance, but they are mostly stem and thorns with a few blooms and a dark background."

The *Sense and Sensibility* artwork includes curling pen lines, as Audrey wanted to remind readers of the way Austen would have written these books, "by hand, with a dip pen. In my original art the hands were greenish, corpselike, but Penguin asked for more lively hands as they thought the green might be off-putting to gentle readers." The portrait of Austen on the inside back flaps is based on an engraving of the author.

The *Sense and Sensibility* cover went through several ideas, looking for an image that would convey the book's "balance between reason and turbulence", as Audrey describes it. These representations of the novel's contrasting Dashwood sisters proved to be either too extreme for the publisher – including the two women with cut-out medical engravings of a brain and heart for their heads: "Jane Austen meets Max Ernst" – or too sweet. Finally, Audrey realised she needed to take another approach. "I've got to abandon this notion of depicting these characters. How does this thing feel, really? And I decided that what it feels like is this very big, emotional tempest happening in this tiny constrained, domestic scene. So I ended up, literally, with a tempest in a teacup." The cup and saucer chosen to be depicted in the artwork have a personal connection to the artist, having belonged to her great grandmother.

Some elements were adjusted on the final versions of both published covers (the original artwork colours are shown here), with the background colours enhanced to brighten the yellow and pink colours. Audrey felt the commissions had been a good collaborative experience and, as part of a series of covers taking an irreverent approach to their titles' contents, her artwork encourages a fresh interpretation of two classic novels.

Audrey Niffenegger lives in the USA.

Shaun Tan
Eric

Eric is one of 15 stories from *Tales From Outer Suburbia*, a collection written and illustrated by Shaun Tan. "I've always loved anthologies of very short stories, I think because they can closely reflect my experiences and memories of the real world, which tend to be more fragmentary than continuous." Whether graphic novels or storybooks, Shaun's work holds universal appeal yet with strong autobiographical aspects and personal emotions at the core. The narratives in this collection share an impression of childhood within an ordinary suburban world, experienced as magical, sometimes scary, "or", as Shaun says, "just plain strange, which I think any childhood is!" He refers to "real-life memories" here, in this five-page story, remembering a foreign houseguest whose awkward presence and quietness left him and his wife feeling, "a little perplexed and sometimes anxious".

The metaphorical content within these images allows the story to transcend cultural barriers that may otherwise limit its appreciation and, importantly, allows the story to resonate with a broad audience. Eric is a mysterious, two-dimensional character dwarfed by the monumental situations he has been placed in – the sense of his alienation is tangible. "A lot of my work is like this, it's very metaphorical, but I don't contemplate that so much while working at my desk. I'm just trying to 'convince' myself that everything looks and feels 'right'. Of course, you can say that his absence of features has something to do with a communication

Eric, a short story from
Tales From Outer Suburbia, Shaun Tan,
published by Allen & Unwin, Australia, 2009

"It's been a constant surprise throughout my career, how strongly people relate to these often very idiosyncratic images and stories. Arguably it's their specific peculiarity that makes them a shared, somehow familiar experience."

From **Tales From Outer Suburbia**, Shaun Tan,
published by Allen & Unwin, Australia, 2009

problem, and so they are metaphorical. But at the end of the day it's not necessary to think about these things consciously."

The story is conveyed through words and text, and the stylistic visual approach is an important factor in the communication process. The realism of these images contributes to the credibility of the idiosyncratic character and his situations. As Shaun reveals, "this must not be seamless" – there is a conscious emphasis of texture and subtle mark-making so that the audience is aware that they are reading drawings. This stylisation is therefore functional, "we might forget the metaphorical nature – the basic unreality. Everything needs to feel as if it is in quotation marks, both real and unreal at the same time."

The format in which text and image interact is also conceptually purposeful, creating a particular visual journey. This spread adopts a convention used commonly in graphic novels: frames grouped together seen as one unified whole, a "single thematic moment", rather than frames of sequential action, i.e. incidents that can also be read autonomously and separately. This formation adds to the message. "The common idea that emerges from their grouping is the absurd scale difference. We realise that all of these visitor activities are 'too big' for this little guy."

As author and illustrator Shaun controls the interconnection of both words and imagery. One function is relative to the other, and paring down each is an objective. "In short, strange stories like this, it's

very important to preserve the enigmatic nature of the experience by keeping both words and images minimal, allowing the reader a lot of room to use their imagination and openly speculate."

The minimal text works with contrasting images, dense with detail. They work together without duplication. "The style of writing is very simple and matter-of-fact, full of descriptive gaps. The pictures are quite descriptive, but full of explanatory gaps. I guess these deliberate omissions reduce any distraction from the main aspect of the narrative." The spaces allow us to focus on feeling and to actively interpret, and, "in doing so, I think we end up feeling more involved with the story, ironically because it says so little."

Shaun says that there was a cathartic dimension to writing and illustrating this story, in that he too has exhibited behaviours similar to Eric. "I realised after the fact that this story is actually about me, about my life as an artist. I have a tendency to react to experience very indirectly or internally, in a way that can occasionally frustrate others – being passively observant rather than active." Eric's glorious gift of a colourful garden left in the pantry after his silent departure is captivating. As Shaun says, "It just happens that some people are not outwardly emotionally expressive and might communicate better in other ways." This is a metaphor in itself. Shaun's illustrations, books like this, and the multi-award-winning graphic novel *The Arrival* have also been received worldwide with justified rapture.

Shaun Tan lives in Australia.

> "Being able to control the process from start to finish and having full responsibility for the final result is the advantage in practising comics."
> Asaf Hanuka

Asaf and Tomer Hanuka
The Dirties

The Dirties is a short story, told in graphic novel format, published as part of a collection of stories by Meathaus books. Words combine with images, with pages constructed from panels to tell an extraordinary story.

This piece was self-generated in concept and approach, reflecting the aesthetic dogma of the publisher in which experimentation within the boundaries of the short-comic fiction format is encouraged. Gangs of uniformed children oddly inhabit a nightmarish, industrial landscape. With no apparent adult supervision the ambience is tense with a sense of escalating menace.

A compelling dimension of this piece is that it is the product of two illustrators, twin brothers Asaf and Tomer Hanuka, working collaboratively. With the foundation of a shared childhood immersed in the fantasy world of comic books and in drawing together, activities that offered entertainment and escape, their now parallel illustration careers occasionally merge, as they did for The Dirties. Given this background it is unsurprising that, as Asaf says, "comics come naturally".

The particular way that graphic novels function and carry a narrative is quite different from other forms of illustrative fiction. As Tomer says, "It forces the reader to find a connection within his own thought in a given moment, putting himself in the action while trying to find a solution for what is disguised as a riddle." This fusion of imagery and text, and their relative functions, is key to carrying the narrative. A graphic novel empowers the viewer as a partner in the storytelling process. Asaf confirms the importance of the space occupied by the audience, what he describes as, "the gap between words and pictures", describing this as, "the tension that makes comics worth reading; a major tool in every cartoonist's toolbox".

Having worked collaboratively on the award-winning animated film Waltz with Bashir, the brothers recognise that with its dramatic viewpoints, deliberate pacing and careful framing there is also a strong cinematic feel in this work. They acknowledge that specific angles were inspired by cinematic language and the iconic images of old printed posters: "We will use whatever codes have been created in the cinematic language for our own purpose, as long as it fits the narrative."

Full-page spread from **The Dirties**, written and illustrated by Asaf and Tomer Hanuka, Meathuas, 2009. *The Dirties* is available as a free online download

Full-page spread from **The Dirties**,
written and illustrated by Asaf
and Tomer Hanuka, published by
Meathaus SOS, 2009

Given their work within animation balancing text and image in the storytelling process, whether or not the narrative takes on other dimensions when animated, is an interesting consideration. "Many times the medium dictates the content, maybe not the plot points, but something deeper in the essence of any story which is strongly intertwined with the way it's told," says Asaf. Tomer adds, "We are not interested in creating a storyboard for a possible production. On the contrary, if someone was to invite us to create the story as animation, I'm sure it'd be a completely different animal as these are such different mediums."

With its crisp lines, snatched viewpoints and considered detail, the technical realism of The Dirties contributes to the unsettling nature of the piece. They convincingly create a disturbing world that Tomer says, "could exist and that the viewer trusts you enough to explore for a little while." This visual description of a place is bound functionally with the narrative. It is laden with symbolic meaning, what Asaf refers to as, "telling the emotional story: depicting the internal state under the pretext of showing the external landscape." Tomer suggests that the drama and fantasy of the piece is heightened because the world is seen from the viewpoint of children. The saturated colour is also used strategically, becoming an integral dimension of the narrative: "the violence eventually grows from the 'safe' parts, the pink, bright places – reality sneaking up on the fantasy."

The illustrators reveal that although not based on one specific incident the piece has an autobiographical dimension, depicting an environment similar to that in which they grew up in Israel. Tomer explains that the troubling story has its roots in their own lives. "The plot is an extreme version of our childhood in a way." He adds, "Looking back at it, and thinking about what was going on in the world around 2000–2008 with the Iraq war – there is a part of it that I think deals directly with those confused emotions." Asaf infers that there was a cathartic dimension to the piece, adding, "the motivation in writing and illustrating a story is never to convey a message, but to find relief from dark corners of one's personal past."

This graphic novel is authorial work at its best: although intended for publication The Dirties is without compromise or inhibition a vehicle for a story the brothers wanted to tell. Asaf says, "By forming and creating via that dark substance one can reach the light. In that sense the motivation for creation is first of all personal and doesn't regard a possible exterior reaction." Tomer says, "As for the collaboration, it's a bit like working against one's automatic intuition, and it's a good way to examine your own instincts."

Twin brothers **Asaf** and **Tomer Hanuka** were born in Israel, where Asaf continues to live and work. Tomer now lives and works in New York, USA.

"I did quite a lot of stage design in my young days, and I think that is also a big help in illustration because you can't help picking up the theatrical tricks of scale and movement."

Jan Pieńkowski
The Thousand Nights and One Night

ntricate silhouettes of castles and forests, heroines, wicked villains and mythical creatures illustrate the many tales that Jan Pieńkowski has illuminated since the 1970s. The strong compositional elements are highlighted by the vivid and decorative backgrounds upon which the silhouetted figures and landscapes sit. Observation and figure drawing has always been an important element of his craft. "At the age of 15 my father sent me to a life class, and I have persevered with life drawing ever since." (Indeed, for 35 years he has held a life class every week in his studio.) "It may be a bit of a slog, but it makes a difference to the illustrations"

The Thousand Nights and One Night, a retelling by Jan's partner, David Walser, of Shahrazade's gripping tales revealed night after night to King Shahryar, was reissued in 2011 and continues Jan's signature silhouette style. Approaching the concept for the cover artwork, Jan had to "consider the idea of all the different stories, because it is such a famous anthology of stories". The black palace, with glowing windows revealing characters representing the various stories told by Shahrazade, proved to be the solution.

Born in Poland, Jan had these tales read to him as a boy, and was brought up on English books during the Second World War (Polish ones were forbidden). He read his grandparents' books, which included Rudyard Kipling stories. "So I had a notion of 'the East'. I had this idea that it existed like that, some of the books had illustrations as well, and they stuck in my mind. I knew there was a place like that."

Children often appreciate fiction when it is illustrated with conviction, and to seek authentic reference for David's retelling they travelled to the Middle East, "and other lands where these stories might have come from," says Jan. "And I drew from life, I drew the people as best I could, the things they wore – and still do – very elaborate clothes and so on. And then of course the wonderful buildings, especially the palaces and the mosques, and to some extent the trees." The shapes of the palace's domes in the artwork are not strictly accurate, but nevertheless are based on buildings he drew in situ. Jan has a strong affinity with countryside, having lived in it for much of his life. Various trees and plants are often placed in the illustrations, and the tree growing inside the palace was drawn during a stop in a village where Jan spotted a tree tied with prayer ribbons inside a dusty yard. "I love doing the trees. And I suppose they are made up, but because I notice things they are probably made up reasonably accurately. I do it from observation, I never do it from life."

Iran's unexpectedly dramatic landscapes inspired the cover's torn-paper background mountains, "So there

The Thousand Nights and One Night
Written by David Walser and illustrated by Jan Pieńkowski,
Puffin Books, 2007 and 2011

you are in the capital, in a grimy city, and then one day the grime lifts up and you suddenly see the wonderfully snowy mountains, as if you'd seen them in Windsor. So I put those in there."

Collaboration with the designer is an important factor in children's publishing, and Jan worked closely with his art director on this cover, drawing various elements for the picture and selecting the best ones to bring together for the final image. A version of the cover artwork is also used as the title page with the art director rearranging the elements, reversing some to reshape the composition.

In the past, Jan's silhouettes would be placed over his own hand-marbled papers, as in the *Fairy Tales* artwork, shown here. Now, "of course," he says, "with the computer you can do these very spectacular skies, which would have been very unnerving if you did them the old-fashioned way. You just needed to make one mistake, and that was it."

Interior illustrations for *The Thousand Nights and One Night* are either black on white, or bordered with patterns and set on coloured backgrounds, some of which were sourced from the Science Museum library of immense enlargements of structures, and one from the photograph of the underside of a bus-stop shelter roof. He hopes these unusual patterns "convey the richness and the alienness of this part of the world".

The enduring popularity, since the 1970s, of Jan's silhouette artwork is easily attributed to its aesthetic qualities and the timelessness of folk stories from the past. But in much of his work he has kept away from details which would tie the characters to any specific modern time, removing detail and stylising features. "I work in a kind of limbo. It's not exactly 'now', most of the time."

Jan Pieńkowski was born in Poland and lives in the UK.

Aladdin's Lamp
Interior illustration, The Thousand Nights and One Night, 2011

Fairy Tales
Jan Pieńkowski and David Walser, Puffin Books, 1975 and 2005

> "I really like the challenge of rethinking the whole process of the book."

Sara Fanelli
The Onion's Great Escape

Children have enquiring minds, and Sara Fanelli's book *The Onion's Great Escape* sets out to encourage responses to some philosophical questions in a novel way. A young onion's quest to escape the frying pan through growing wise, learning to question and doubt, is echoed by a physical escape from her possible fate through a removable perforated central onion shape in the book. Publisher Phaidon proposed a book which 'disappears', one which when finished is different from when started, "I found that really inspiring," she says, "because I like exploring what you can do with the book form."

The character of the onion had surfaced in her previous publications, with Sara enjoying the feel of the onion shape, combined with the gesture of making its curved marks; so in this new book she developed the layers of the story of the onion's journey to liberation with reference to the peeling of this vegetable. This journey has two levels, the escape from the chopping knives and frying pan (also the book), and the growth of the onion through asking questions. The book recognises that children naturally query the world around them, and may debate moral issues and decisions, "Of course," observes Sara, "we put this word 'philosophy' over it." The questions posed throughout are not easy, so she felt the story should echo that; the imagery where the knives start slicing the onion heroine is quite daring. "I wanted it not to be too sweet in general. Otherwise, it's a bit false."

A friendly command, 'Think! Imagine! And Write!', appears early in the book, whose participatory nature is part of its strength, stimulating responses to the unanswered questions in the text. "It's nice to have a book only of questions. So every reply is good – it's not right and wrong," and, with space designated on various pages for readers to write their replies, Sara intends the book to become a personal journal, as it is only completed "once the owner makes their mark". She imagines that once the child has grown up, the written answers will serve as an intriguing reminder of how the reader thought as their younger self, answering, 'Can you forget to remember?' and 'Is something less real because we cannot touch it?' in the context of questions on 'memory' and 'fear', and the moral teaser, 'Is it as bad as doing a bad deed if you do nothing when someone needs help?'

The warmth of handwritten text in pencil, ink and felt-tip serves as an encouragement to write in the book without fear of being too neat, aided by the texture of the uncoated paper, which deliberately invites mark-making. The tactile pleasure of removing the onion shape, page by page, acts as a reward to the child for

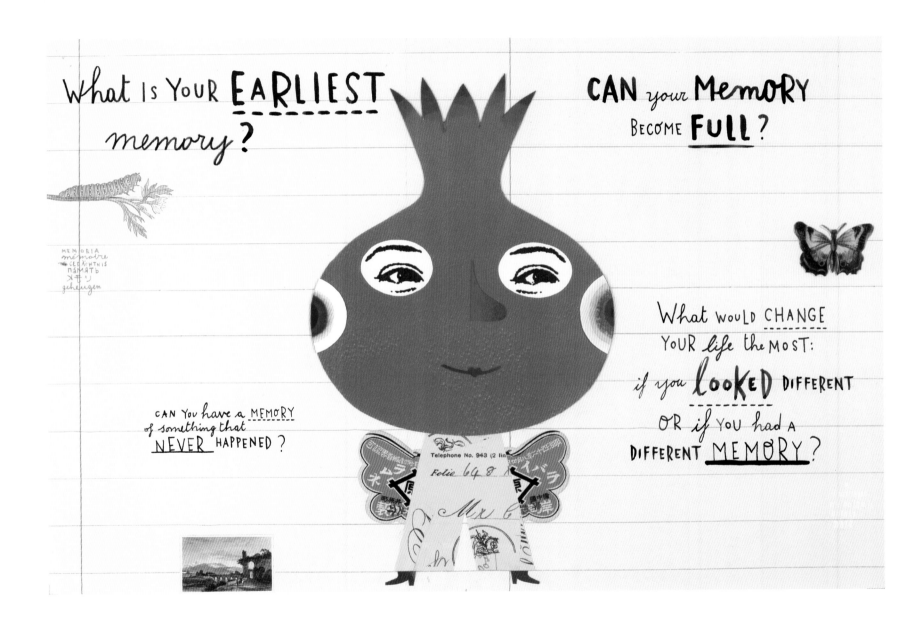

The Onion's Great Escape
Written and illustrated by Sara Fanelli, published by Phaidon, 2012

Sometimes I Think, Sometimes I Am by Sara Fanelli, published by Tate Publishing, 2007. The character of the onion was developed by the illustrator through earlier works. The narrative was later built around the concept using an evolved version as the central character

writing in the book. This physicality is an important element of the publication for Sara, prompting interaction between reader and book.

Sara works in collage, to print scale, and this method feeds in to her love of old things – "I'm addicted to the past, and I'm addicted to old stationery. I find it rich – it has narratives" – while collected materials such as yellowing accountancy slips carry some of the less obvious references in the artwork ("to give and to take"), adding to the story's layers. Found photographs are also included, with several introducing a humorous element to the incidental pleasures of small images and words scattered throughout the pages.

Technically, the book was complicated to plan, with the central removable section always a consideration in the page design, being required to work on the page and also as a separated element. Text in this central space of the layout is often in bold letterpress, alternating with the onion's face to make sure that there is variety in the many folds of the stand-alone onion once 'escaped' from the book. Cut-out monoprints are also incorporated, with Sara often wiping the inks on the plate before printing, to enhance the textures.

What happens to the removed onion-shaped central section? "I'd love to see where they end up," muses Sara, "I was imagining it'd be good if you need to keep children busy during a car journey, the fact that this might get taken on holiday ..."

Sara recognises that the developments of this book have seen her work continue to mature, and with three-dimensionality contributing to the current diversity of the book form, *The Onion's Great Escape* offers an experience for the brain and the hands, asking young readers to weigh up conundrums and, unusually, literally pull the book apart.

Sara Fanelli was born in Italy and lives in the UK.

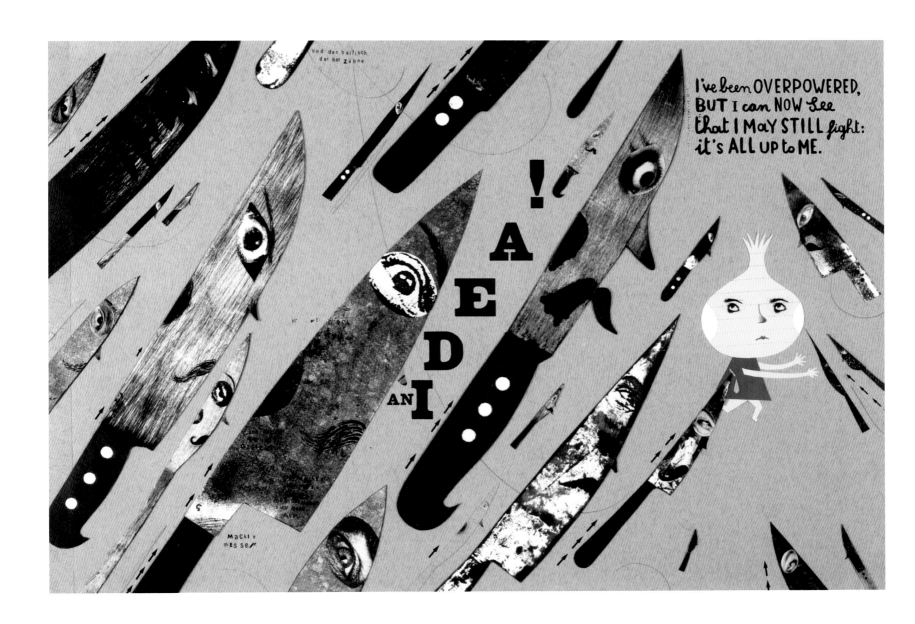

The Onion's Great Escape
Written and illustrated by Sara Fanelli, published by Phaidon, 2012

Kadir Nelson
Heart and Soul: The Story of America and African Americans

Encompassing the history of a nation through a significant element of its population requires breadth and detail. Kadir Nelson both wrote and illustrated *Heart and Soul: The Story of America and African Americans*, creating an accessible history with an intimate feel, narrated by an elderly woman – a former slave – addressing the younger generation on the trials and triumphs of African Americans through one family, from colonial days through to the civil rights movement and more recent significant events.

For the images to relate closely to the text, Kadir wanted *Heart and Soul* to have the feeling of an old scrapbook or family album. "The images serve as reference points to the narrator's family story, whether as family photos, period photographs, or historical images." The historical scope of the book and the nature of the imagery demanded that research was undertaken for each picture. Whilst creating the illustrations Kadir sourced old American period paintings and photographs for reference, using them as style guides for much of the artwork – specifically for the paintings of Pap, George Washington, those depicting the soldiers of the Civil War and World War II, and the civil rights images. The actual historical paintings appearing within the artwork add an additional element of gravitas and connection to the past.

The book's story follows the life of Pap, the narrator's grandfather, from his capture and enslavement as a young child in Africa in the 1800s up to her own witnessing of Dr Martin Luther King's 'I have a dream' speech in 1963, and her casting of a vote for the first African American president. The images anchor the text in the personal, and this one of Young Pap introduces a character with a determined countenance whose quiet strength is echoed through the story. "Facial expressions, posture, hand positioning, composition, lighting, palette – all of these are very deliberate choices that help tell a story," says Kadir. "I enjoy using all of these devices to heighten the drama or play on the subtlety of each subject."

The mirrored composition looks at the young boy from the ankles up, the cropping of his feet a deliberate emphasis. "Pap is a man-child. The low angle adds to his power and character and shows his dominance over his dire situation." The rich blue sky and shadowed lighting give the figure solidity, dignity and presence. Light is an important element in the book's paintings, often purposefully heightening the drama of a scene, depicted with a soft, warm glow. To capture this Kadir used both natural and controlled lighting when taking his own reference photographs, or relied on his imagination if required.

Young Pap
From **Heart and Soul: The Story of America and African Americans**
Written and illustrated by Kadir Nelson, published by Balzer + Bray, 2011

Brave Children
At Little Rock, Arkansas, USA, with a troops escort to school
From **Heart and Soul: The Story of America and
African Americans**

Dr Martin Luther King Jr.
Giving his 'I have a dream' speech at Washington D.C., USA
From **Heart and Soul: The Story of America and
African Americans**

Slave Ship
From **Heart and Soul: The Story of America and African Americans**

Kadir used himself as a model for many of the figures in the illustrations, and his family took part for several images. His neighbour's son posed for Young Pap. "I photographed him and combined it with photo reference of myself and historical photographs of children for this painting." This combination of sources brings a convincing sense that the characters throughout the book were real people based on Kadir's family's past. Although Pap is a fictional character and represents children who were enslaved in the antebellum South, he didn't necessarily think of Pap as an 'every-child', "To me he represents the last slave in my family whose name I never knew. *Heart and Soul* is a very personal story for me as it is made up of several of my family stories, along with tales from other families like mine."

Along with the image of Young Pap, there are many striking compositions underpinning the book's illustrations, and Kadir continues the richness of colour and vivid contrast of light and shade throughout, often utilising a foreground element to frame the compositions, such as in *Brave children, Little Rock, Arkansas*, where the integration of schoolchildren in white schools necessitated armed guards. Here soldiers are shown foregrounded in deep shadow. Working as visual development artist on Steven Spielberg's film, *Amistad*, he was inspired by the director's framing devices and has brought this into the structure of his images.

The detail and gravitas of the artwork in *Heart and Soul* combine with the text to produce a book which conveys the journey of the narrator's family with compassion and a strong sense of atmosphere.

Kadir Nelson lives in the USA.

"My goal is to inform viewers in a way that is very familiar to them – the significance of citizenship and how American and African American historical achievements, both large and small, have helped to create a national platform that allows for freedom, and the right to fight for it."

Kleenex glory/failure
Kleenex (Kimberly-Clark Company),
2010. For JWT advertising agency, UK

Gail Armstrong
Feelings – Kleenex campaign

The multilayered nature of Gail's work can be seen as a metaphor for the creative approach and intention she brings to her work. Working across the field of illustration, her practice embodies a depth of involvement, conceptually and aesthetically, in the service of a multitude of international clients. Here, revealing the power of illustration to sell a product and assert a brand, Gail offers insights into the process of working within an advertising context, demonstrating the distinction between a conceptual and a purely aesthetic interpretation of a brief. "There are almost two types of client. Those who want a lot of my creative input, who trust, without a lot of back and forth discussion, how it develops. With the others I am more tightly pinned down with not much scope conceptually. That's where I see myself as a paper sculptor and expect my job to make the concept beautiful and the best it can be."

The pieces chosen here demonstrate the kind of work for which Gail has earned both recognition and respect, and are evidence of the ongoing power of images to sell a product through its ideas and messages – the objective of this series of illustrations being to promote the brand, and ultimately to sell Kleenex tissues. As commissioned pieces of advertising they are the symbiosis of both her ideas and those of Christiano Neves, the Creative Director from JWT with whom she worked on the commission; as such, they demonstrate the particular and complex relationships between creatives in the advertising industry. She reflects, "I think a large part of my skill as an illustrator is in interpreting what the client requires and then making it work visually," recalling of her working relationship with Neves, "We thought along a similar vein. We developed each other's ideas. I could see what he wanted and added an extra layer, honing his ideas and making them work across the set."

In advertising, the process of communicating with the audience is complex. These often humorous narratives are intended to connect using the universal appeal of opposites and a shared understanding of the significance of the depicted events in the context of the product. They epitomise and parody archetypally recognised fantasies about getting married, being a famous footballer and enjoying celebrity as a pop star. As well as the use of stereotyped characters, Gail paid attention to the formal visual elements of composition, colour and tone, vitally symbolic ingredients with immediate narrative and emotional connotations, as befitting a product associated with emotional highs and lows.

Although the impact of gender in the success of illustration is scarcely explored, the invisible ingredient

Kleenex yes/no
Kleenex (Kimberly-Clark Company),
2010.
JWT advertising agency, UK.

in this work is the female perspective Gail provides – the humour that softens the more male approach to the interpretation of the brief. The subsequent irony infusing the pieces is pivotal to the campaign and its consequent success.

There is a consistency across this set of pieces that formulates the sense of product identity, visually as well as conceptually. Evolving narratives are common, successful approaches within advertising, and campaigns such as this one can offer a rewarding opportunity for an illustrator to bring depth to a given idea. Gail reflects on the gains of working on such interconnecting yet separate images, revealing, "one image with impact is great, but working with sets of images with a story developing through more than one is what I really like. You get to reach into it."

There is a danger that association with high-profile advertising campaigns can stymie an illustrator's career. Equally damaging can be the temptation to typecast an illustrator on the basis of their technique. Gail's paper-based work is a reminder to look beyond the superficial and technical qualities of any piece of illustration or design. When she talks of perspectives and depth and layers she is referring not to the qualities of the papers that she carefully selects but the processes and ideas inherent in her images. Gail draws a parallel with earlier stages of her career when her practice included graphic design and photography. "I was aware even when working in two dimensions of constructing with elements, with some things receding and others advancing. I always think in three dimensions. It's a way of looking and a way of thinking as well as a way of working."

Gail Armstrong was born in Scotland and lives in England.

"I don't see myself as a paper sculptor, I think of myself as a communicator. I hope people choose me not because of what I can do with paper but because of the 'extra something' that I add as an illustrator."

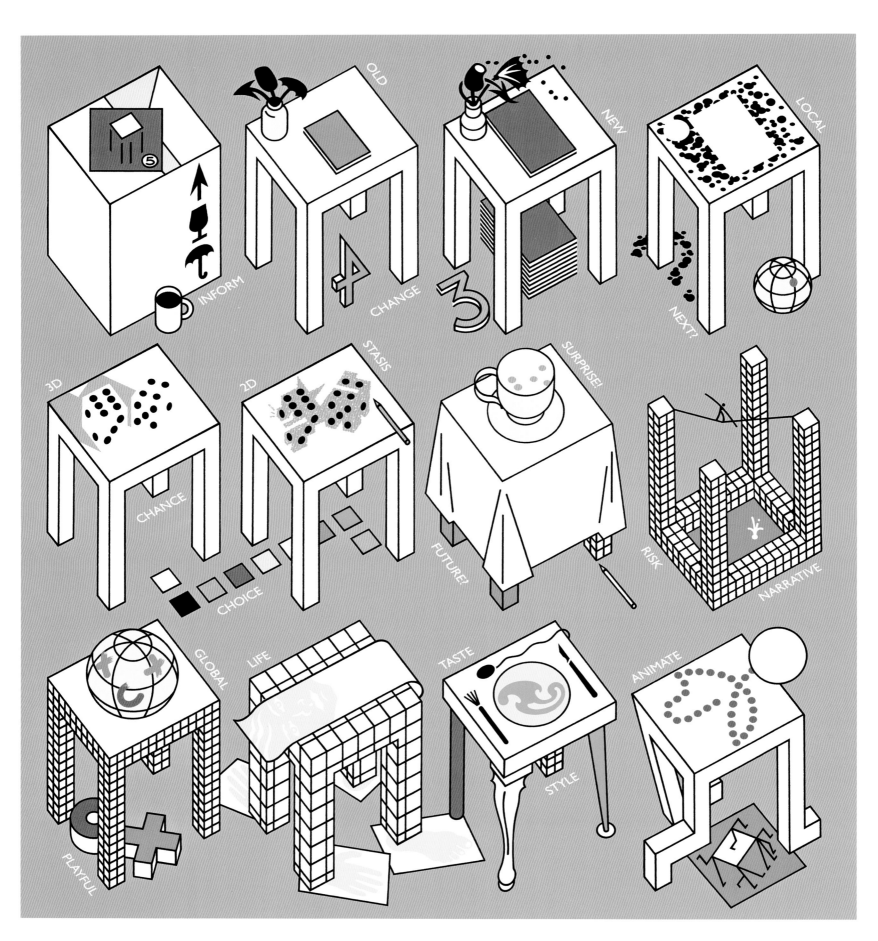

"If you're an uptight illustrator like me, it's not about having fun, it's about getting it exactly where you want it."

George Hardie
Turning the Tables editorial

Magazine covers require an image that catches the eye and also intrigues, and George Hardie's *Turning the Tables* illustration does both. With a narrative that leads the viewer over twelve permutations of a simple white table, the image cleverly illustrates the theme of that issue of *Varoom*: Change.

The tables sequence related to George's longstanding interest in spot-the-difference pictures. "If you're doing what 'change' means in a particular subject, you've probably got to have chapter headings, and that's the first step." These headings, placed by each table, can then be played with, "It's very like a game really, in the sense that you're seeing how playful you can be. It's like variations in music – a musician is trying something a hundred different ways." And as he is asking the viewer to participate in a game, their reward is in discovering the links between the words and images: "That's the principle of it." This interlocking content is good value for the viewer, offering something that requires some unravelling, "It's a bit of a cheat in a way. You know if you put a lot of work into something, it's likely to be more interesting."

He comments that the proportion of time taken to develop the idea – "always the tricky thing" – is almost longer than that spent on drawing. Here, once the table was conceived as the main element, George liked the idea of commencing the image with it in a box, "then off we went, really". Twelve permutations were decided on – "I couldn't have the fun I had with that if I only did four" – and then time was spent working on the differences and connections among the chain of tables. He believes that a drawing is built, constructed from various elements, and "if those elements are bricks they're still movable". He finds it "an enjoyable struggle" to get the image how he wants it, ensuring the narrative of the image tells the story in the best way within the composition. The magazine cover dimensions are the first point to consider, and to make the space work for the image was "obvious in this. It all feeds round and round."

Clues from each table lead the viewer to the connection with the next one, with symbols from the box – "I've used those in so many ways, I really love them" – re-forming as 'flowers' which then go on to spread 'pollen' across to the following table. The tightrope-walker table was inspired by the documentary about Philippe Petit,

Turning the Tables
Varoom magazine cover, issue 16, published by the Association of Illustrators, 2011

who walked between the World Trade Center buildings in 1974, and also as George knew one table was going to have to be upside down, "because that's a really strong 'turning of the tables'." There is also a cheeky reference to Hockney's painting *A Bigger Splash*: "A smaller splash," he smiles. *Varoom* magazine is for a visually literate audience of illustrators and designers, and George kept that in mind. "I quite like everyone to feel that one of their preoccupations about how 'change' is going to be is covered in there."

As George doesn't use a computer himself for artwork, drawn elements are scanned and put together by a colleague, essential for an image such as this. "It won't be the same if I draw it 18 times by hand. It's better to build on one. Also, it remains changeable up to the last possible minute." Colour is added digitally and adjusted through printed samples of the image.

Text is an integral part of George's practice, and is utilised across *Turning the Tables* as 'headings', running from *Inform* at the beginning to *Animate*, beside the final table, transforming into a figure poised to run. It is there for several purposes. "It's partly to give yourself one more element, to break things up and fill awkward spaces and so on, which I quite often do with some trick like that. And partly to help people to understand it – or the opposite. You can either say 'this is a pipe' or 'this isn't a pipe', and that's useful."

The three-dimensional isometric view of many of George's images suits the repetition of this picture and comes, he says, from having to find a way to draw. "I learned it in geometrical mechanical drawing at school because I wasn't good enough at Latin. So I can't claim any ownership to it at all!" He enjoys the opportunities the isometric view presents to reveal more, "because it's got three sides to everything, which is brilliant".

George Hardie lives in the UK.

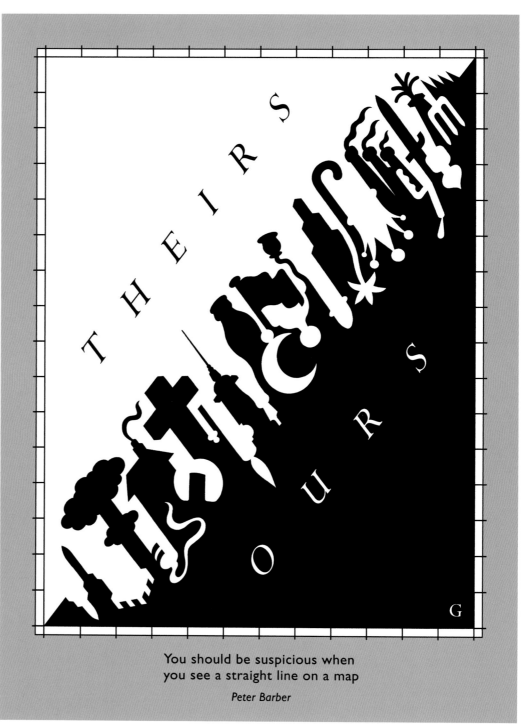

You should be suspicious when you see a straight line on a map

Peter Barber

Examples of other commissions, above and opposite:
'You should be suspicious when you see a straight line on a map'
Illustration for *Nozone IX*, USA, Empire edition.
Client: Nicholas Blechman, 2004

The History of English Gardening
Invitation card to The Garden Show, Stansted Park, UK.
Client: The Garden Show, 1994

Nelson Beer label image
Client: Taboo Group, Melbourne, Australia, 2008

*"We take things forward
in each brief."*

WeBuyYourKids
Nelson Beer label

There is a hint of something slightly sinister emanating from the bold character staring out from the beer bottle, a quality that is an often recognisable ingredient in the work of Australian duo, WeBuyYourKids (WBYK). This image has an essence of the freer, more personal work for which Biddy Maroney and Sonny Day have become renowned. It combines a strong craft aesthetic with suggestions of deeper and often darker symbolic content, pulled together here not simply to sell beer but also to convey a message that becomes part of the brand identity. "Mystery is the real word," Sonny says, "the keyword given by the client."

WBYK describe themselves as "commercial illustrators – we draw for money." Their images are used famously as album covers, poster art, for websites and advertising, and the partners display a chameleon-like adaptability whilst retaining a particular identity. "We've pushed ourselves and will never be stuck with one defined style. We take things forward in each brief." This attitude requires open-minded clients receptive to new discovery. Sonny recounts that, "nine out of ten times we're allowed to keep moving and the people we work for get something they can call their own – they're part of the journey."

He recalls that they were initially restrained in response to this particular brief. "The beer already had a name and we were working around that. We were playing it safe with our original ideas." He laughs. "We couldn't even mention death!" Pushed by the client in the second round of visuals to "have fun", their final design is a striking piece of contemporary gothic, the white figure stark against the traditional brown bottle, a vintage icon with a contemporary twist.

This piece demonstrates the momentum injected by self-generated work in any creative "journey" and the esoteric interests that continue to nourish such commissioned pieces, on many levels. "We're very lucky that we're hired, for the most part, to draw things based on our private work, so we experience art and business in a fairly seamless way." Intriguingly, Sonny says, "Our own stuff has more menace to it and we want to reflect a little of that meaning. It's a bit dark." At the time of this commission they were, "both into witches, fairytales and certain mythological characters". They grew up loving horror movies and comic books, the escapism of fantasy and mysticism, although they describe what they do as "making embedded meaning".

Sonny accepts that they are limited by what can be conveyed in static, one-off illustrations, that they put symbols into the work, "not too consciously". He describes them as "the ideas", explaining, "it's the images that speak".

In this image the character with his top hat is reminiscent of voodoo; there are symbols on the chest, question marks, and is that a drop of blood on the hat? As Sonny explains, "It's the quality of the meaning in the symbols that we take forward in more commercial work – we're investing new meaning". To clarify, he says, "Lots of symbols are amazing but not appropriate for selling beer!"

The ambiguity is deliberate, to draw in an audience who will be both attracted to and intrigued by the product. "We don't want to dictate what people do or don't get in our work. Everyone reacts differently and I enjoy that part. I don't want to spell it out." The partners are phenomenally prolific yet fastidious in their range, but Sonny reiterates the importance of having fun with their ideas, laughingly revealing that, "'Camp' is a word we like to describe our work!"

WBYK enjoy the physical and organic nature of the process. As a result, the work for which they are well recognised often has a tactile quality, an implied sense of tradition that may have been strategically brought to this new product. "The craft is something we try to incorporate. We like it to have a feel that it could be screenprinted. We do it and embrace the mistakes. If the look shows in digital-made work, we're happy."

Although promotional work created for bands (such as the images opposite created for CD packaging for The Laurels) is a substantial part of their practice, their expansive and eclectic folio is also charged by an extra force, the music that is the soundtrack to and "a gigantic part of both of our lives." This also exerts an invisible and maybe indefinable impact upon the image. "A lot of music drives our ideas, whatever we're listening to."

The Nelson Beer label is evidence of the need for intelligent commissioning by designers who are able to read the work of the illustrators they commission, harnessing their defining qualities whilst encouraging and optimising creative freedom and integrity. As Sonny summarises, "often ideas get shut down quickly – we don't always get the chance to spread our wings and flesh an idea out."

WeBuyYourKids – Biddy Maroney and Sonny Day
– live and work in Australia.

Nelson Beer
Client: Taboo Group, Melbourne Australia, 2008

CD packaging for the band The Laurels, 2012

Reportage
Topography
Narrative – A Sense Of Place
Information Communication

02 Documentary

Artworks can document or report upon an expansive variety of issues and situations, presenting a viewpoint which can only be revealed through research and skill in composing, in fields such as reportage, medical, historical reconstruction and information illustration. Documentary illustration can aid understanding, expanding and extending areas of specialist knowledge that sometimes can't be easily revealed in any other way.

Reportage and topographical illustration can offer a unique perspective on events and situations, providing a distinct sense of place. Reportage is the visual recording of an ongoing or contained situation, event or view of the human condition, often across a series of images, illuminating what is being depicted. Reportage artists can act as witnesses to the extraordinary and the mundane, documenting aspects of contemporary life and culture, revealing aspects of, or offering a new perspective on, familiar worlds or those which have previously been alien to the viewer. In a lens-saturated world where media images bombard us through the TV, press and internet, illustration is overtly a human interpretation of an event, offering a distinctive, individual form of engagement that contributes uniquely to the power of the image.

Working in this area of illustration requires observational power, an involvement with the subject and a willingness to engage with an issue that may be emotionally difficult or may involve capturing a fleeting moment, which may nevertheless represent an important happening as it unfolds.

Reportage offers the opportunity to combine perspectives, as George Butler's multiple viewpoints of Tara the elephant demonstrate. His astute and celebratory observations are commercially functional, aesthetic and ecologically significant in raising public awareness.

Veronica Lawlor's topographic images of New Orleans and Anne Howeson's from London's King's Cross reveal, through their expressive interpretation of the physical urban landscape, a sense of the human and how the world changes around its inhabitants, as either natural or manmade forces exert themselves. They reveal

the power of reportage to evoke an emotional response and deliver narratives that articulate issues and ideas that may be difficult to convey through other forms.

There is much which cannot be clearly revealed except through visual interpretation – the complex workings of the human body or an explanation of systems within industry. Information-based illustration can be a highly specialist area of the professional field, requiring the interpretative skills vividly revealed here through the medical illustration of Craig Foster and the information graphics of Peter Grundy. The clarity of communication comes from the use of an individual visual vocabulary that combines aesthetic, intellectual, creative and semiotic knowledge.

Working on architectural digs in the UK, the energetic drawings of Victor Ambrus are a synthesis of archaeology and art offering powerful visualisations of the lives of our predecessors; advancing knowledge and understanding.

Understanding of the value of reportage as a potent form of communication, in translating various forms of narrative is evident in the examples that clearly synthsise observation with imagination. Combining an idiosyncratic interpretation of American history with reportage, the images created by Maira Kalman provide an entertaining reimagining of the lives of past American presidents.

Christopher Corr travels internationally recording both urban and rural landscapes, celebrating cultural diversity. This direct observation becomes absorbed into his vibrant, evocative illustrations, which work with text to complement and help convey narratives.

All of these artists bring an immediacy to their images that is supported by considered approaches to their subjects, with their individual points of view presenting those subjects in a way that is accessible to the viewer: a sympathy through both observation and interpretation.

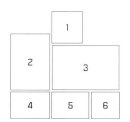

Ecology

The ANGeLS aRe SiNGiNG on this gLoRious Day.

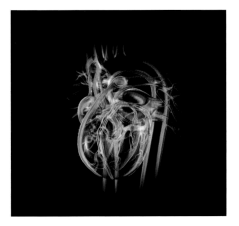

ANA SOLDIER FRISKING
A VILLAGER
APRIL 30, 2011

**Afghan National Army soldier
frisks an old man**
Panjwaii District, Kandahar
Province, 30 April 2011. Sketched
and published on *National Post*
blog the same day.

"I have sketched in any number of seemingly impractical situations. You'd be amazed the places you can sketch."

Richard Johnson
Afghanistan reportage

ichard Johnson has regularly reported in words and images on the conflict in Afghanistan for the Canadian *National Post* and also from Iraq for *The Detroit Free Press*, revealing an evident empathy for his subjects, "I write first person what I see and what I feel about it. I don't have an agenda." Travelling whilst embedded with Canadian or US troops, he considers himself first and foremost to be a journalist, "The drawings are simply a way of getting people to read the story, by getting them to pay attention. I want people to realise what the day-to-day existence is like for our soldiers and the people." His reports are often syndicated through other American newspapers.

Richard is a founder member of the International Society of War Artists, and as well as tours with the army has covered rehabilitation of wounded US Marines left dealing with the consequences of conflicts, and says of his representations of army personnel, "It really helps to know and understand soldiers if you are going to get them to talk to you and be comfortable around you. They have to accept you as worthy of their trust." This image of an Afghan National Army (ANA) soldier frisking an Afghan villager was part of a blog report for the *National Post* about an army

patrol and interaction between the local Afghans, the Canadian soldiers and the ANA. At this point in the campaign, the ANA had taken over much of the soldiering and interaction with the locals as a step towards independence from International Security Assistance Force support, and here they were looking for an elusive local mullah whom they wanted to speak to. "The blog piece is about trust, or the complete lack of it. The Afghans didn't trust the soldiers, and the soldiers didn't trust the Afghans, and the ANA didn't trust the Canadians and vice versa." Although the event may appear mundane, the illustration reveals the tensions between civilian and soldier. "I liked the unique sense of discomfort in the scene. Afghans are very private. Social touching is quite rare. Frisking was uncomfortable for both of them."

Richard's work often features individuals, portraits or small groups of figures, and for him backgrounds can sometimes be considered a distraction from the main subject. This frisking image closely focuses on the two men, giving them equal weight, and required just a few lines to indicate the environment. Context for the scene was provided by the text accompanying the artwork in the *National Post* blog.

Qalat City resident
22 August, 2012

Drawn in Indigo Blue Prismacolour – "The pencil colour is one I fell in love with early in my career" – the image was completed from reference within a couple of hours of the event happening. "I work in one colour because it is all my small brain can handle. I need to create the image as fast as possible – I can't faff around choosing which yellow ochre works with periwinkle blue." Photographic reference will be taken when it is impractical for drawing – "Sometimes there is no opportunity to sketch. I need to be interacting and absorbing everything for the written side of things as well" – but Richard will not work on any image from a photograph after more than 24 hours has passed since taking it.

Through depicting sensitive situations Richard has become adept at being a surreptitious sketcher and photographer. "I am very good at looking like I am looking somewhere else while sketching someone perpendicular to me. It is a bit like big-game hunting. You have to be careful not to spook your quarry." This tactic, he admits, results in many sketchbooks containing pages of unsuccessful, incomplete drawings. Richard's reports have built up to a body of work which encompasses soldiers in action, facing dangers, enduring the boredom in camp and also dealing with the consequences of major injury. Through imagery which brings the viewer closer to situations, he has compiled an enduring record of the unreported aspects of war that most will never encounter, encouraging an empathy with the participants among all those who see his work.

Richard Johnson lives in Canada.

Lance Corporal William Kyle Carpenter
(grenade wounds to head, torso, hands, legs, 2011).
Hunter Holmes McGuire Veterans Affairs Medical Center in Richmond, Virginia, April 2011. Sketched live and published on *National Post* blog a week later.

CORPORAL GABRIEL FERLAND PLAYS TIC-TAC-TOE WITH CHILD IN SALAVAT VILLAGE   MAY 1, 2011

Corporal Gabriel Ferland plays tic-tac-toe in the dirt with a boy in Salavat Village
Panjwaii District, Kandahar Province, 30 April 2011. Sketched and published on *National Post* blog the same day.

Pink Elephant
"I watched her flapping her huge ears, the ends of which were splotched with the palest of pink dots, as if somebody had flicked a paintbrush." For The Elephant Family charity, exhibited for fundraising sale, 2011

George Butler
Tara the Elephant, India reportage

The elephant sways, ears alert and trunk curling around a small branch as she moves towards us. This is one of more than 40 pictures commissioned from George Butler by the Elephant Family charity to document the life of Tara the elephant, the inspiration behind the charity after founder Mark Shand rode her 600 miles across India in the 1970s.

Although still in his twenties, George already embodies the idea of the roving reportager, having undertaken a major road-trip project driving thorough West Africa in 2010, sending drawings back throughout the journey to *The Times* newspaper.

With this image of Tara George aimed to show the power, poise, size and movement of his subject. "The great thing about drawing on location," he says, "is that if you are aware of your subject and confident enough to draw what you see – and not a perception of what you see – then the image will almost certainly convey the character of the subject." The representation of movement can be challenging within a static image, but is something George enjoys documenting, revealing the life in his subject as well as the fact that he was there in front of her – an important element if he is asking the audience to trust the authenticity of what he has drawn.

Prior to travelling to Tara's home in a camp near Kahna National Park, Madhya Pradesh, George researched

the history of conservation and the charity's work in India, then concentrated on the anatomy of the Asian elephant to a point where he could confidently capture characteristics and movements on paper which in real time were only second-long poses. Research is often an important component of reportage work, as George confirms, "I try to have an understanding of context within a subject. Sometimes it works well to be a total outsider, to look at something with fresh eyes." Background investigation here took in the study of jungle life and conservation in relation to the tiger, "something not necessarily relevant to drawing an individual elephant, but which as a reportage project was paramount to empathising with and understanding the context of the drawings". George expanded the project by recording life around the camp and in Delhi, where he spent a couple of days at either end of the trip, drawing the city's inhabitants and architecture.

As the brief required the pictures to be sold for fundraising he was asked to produce large images, as big as A0 down to A4, and these were drawn on paper on a large board with a dip pen and Indian ink. "I try to colour the pictures whilst I am still in front of the subject – but with the heat, and when drawing animals, you are not very often given enough time – and I would have to finish the work afterwards." This process was hampered by systematic power cuts to save electricity, and by Tara's routine, which consisted of eating in the jungle for the entire morning and bathing every

afternoon. Although creating the images at a large size was not a restriction, drawing from life meant that the bigger ones were more difficult – a reminder of the impact and demands the physical environment can exert on reportage work.

Luvkush, Tara's mahout for over twenty years, appears in the drawings and, George comments, "Although we didn't share a common language I think he enjoyed having his pride and joy appreciated. I hope drawing her quickly in pen and ink meant that some of her habits that he recognised as typically 'her' were captured. He almost certainly preferred me drawing Tara than himself!"

George felt this project was a valuable experience. "It has reiterated that I will certainly be doing more of the same work," he says, although he recognises that his next journey will not necessarily be a commissioned project as reportage is not always given due consideration within the commercial illustration market, even in newspapers and magazines. "I'd like to see it used to accompany feature-length articles about subjects which need a new angle or more empathy than perhaps the familiar photography and film shots can provide."

George Butler lives in the UK.

Father and Son
In the village outside Kanha
National Park in Madhya Pradesh,
2011

"I try to have an understanding of context within a subject. Sometimes it works well to be a total outsider, to look at something with fresh eyes."

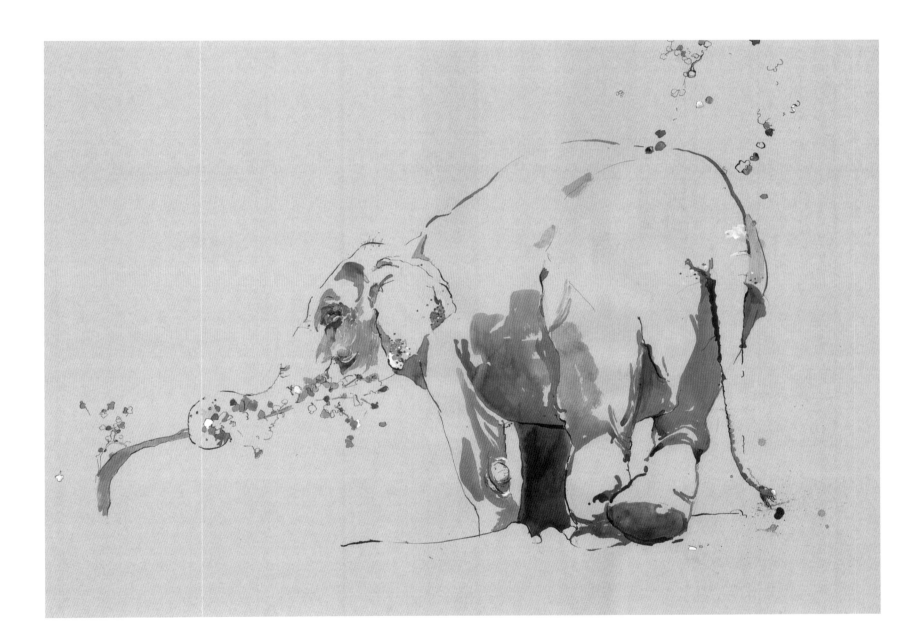

Tara vs Tree
"She positively vibrated with excitement, coiling and uncoiling her trunk like a giant watch spring . . . and uttering sneezes of contentment", 2011

Anne Howeson
Coal and Fish Fictional Future

Although the territory for reportage work can usually be located on a map, memorable work also reflects an internal emotional and intellectual journey. The place at the focus of Anne Howeson's ongoing, largely self-authored work is the central London area of King's Cross. With the huge Victorian train station as its nucleus, its previously sordid, decrepit persona is becoming increasingly gentrified. Witness the glamour of the expansion of direct European train travel, the sophistication of media and culture, and the allure of corporate and commercial transaction. Early on, the prospect of renewal in an area in which Anne lives and feels an affinity for invoked a mixed response in her that infuses the entire project. "I don't have an axe to grind at all. At the beginning of the redevelopment I could see it was going to change out of all recognition and I felt sad. It's an interesting phenomenon to live inside that, and I soon began to feel intrigued and excited. It's fertile ground."

In contrast to the complexity of the lives populating these environments, a sense of calm emanates from this image – a still point in a changing world. The Victorian Coal and Fish Building stands proud, dwarfed by imagined towering constructions stretching through the top of the frame into as yet unseen futures. Its history assigns it monumental status and the foreground trees spread optimistically. This image epitomises the transformation of King's Cross. It is both a commemoration of times past and a suggestion of what the future could hold.

Sorties with a camera into the backstreets, at night, a time of relative emptiness and latent menace, resulted in photographs in which dilapidated buildings, gasometers and building sites were transformed into stage sets by the orange glow of her camera flash. It's an ambience which fed into images such as this one, theatrically documenting the remnants of history whilst "unveiling a fictional future". It may be significant that twilight represents the metamorphosis of one state into another, and it is certain that the work itself occupies a place between physical and psychological geography.

Anne puts herself in her images, not figuratively but expressively and inventively, and the drawings take on an independent life that she nurtures. They communicate on several levels after first resonating with Anne. "They tell me about something else – the unconscious, and it's fascinating. My first scribbles often contain the first thing I want to say but I like refining, it brings out the personality." She reflects on her subconscious personification of some of the jaded buildings she has drawn, referring empathetically to the French writer Apollinaire, who described the Eiffel Tower as "the shepherdess of Paris". "I began drawing people, but it became about the buildings. I'm naturally nostalgic and I started to identify with their plight. They touched me."

The essence of words is often an ingredient of the imagery, contributing to the sense of fiction within the work. Although Anne doesn't specifically seek a literary pulse, King's Cross is alive with the whispering spirits of esteemed writers such as Dickens, Blake and Mary Wollstonecraft, and Anne recognises that new work can often be triggered by a phrase or a memory from a book. Ultimately, she reveals, "I'm listening to my own voice and trying to be honest."

This piece is from the second of three ongoing sets of work created around this theme over a period spanning more than two decades. Certain images have won awards, others have been exhibited, and some published. Given the strongly authorial nature of the imagery Anne didn't strategically embark on the project anticipating these outcomes. "I don't know what I want when I'm working. I often work myself into a state and then I begin to connect with the picture." The opportunity within professional practice to create a breadth of related work within a theme is rare. This reportage project is a reminder of the value to be gained from ongoing personal investigation without the constraints of an external brief.

A sense of this journey being one of openness to discovery is conveyed by a quote from Raymond Carver with which she identifies: "Plot away without hope or expectation."

Anne Howeson was born and lives in the UK.

"I've always been fascinated by people's lives and places that hold people's lives."

Canary Wharf comes to Coal and Fish
Personal work, 2009

Coal and Fish Fictional Future
Twilight in an Unbuilt Place, 2009. Personal work.

Cubitt's Granary
Central St Martins, University of the Arts, 2009. Personal work.

Ninth Ward of New Orleans
Self-initiated project, 2011

"I draw what I see rather than a preconceived idea of what I know."

Veronica Lawlor
New Orleans, Ninth Ward project

The media images of New Orleans being devastated by floods caused by Hurricane Katrina in 2005 are long gone, but the impact of the catastrophe remains – an enduring reminder of lives ruined and communities destroyed. Veronica Lawlor visited the city in 2011 with the optimistic intention of drawing the much-publicised new housing developments, to document encouraging signs of restoration and regeneration. The drawings that she produced instead reflect a more sombre reaction to the real situation she encountered in the Lower Ninth Ward area where the floods had greatest impact. "I was surprised by how much *hadn't* been done. There were huge areas of abandoned fields – the footprints of buildings." The expressive quality in this work shows the potential for reportage illustration to communicate directly within a political and conceptual realm.

New Orleans, for many, is synonymous with a unique aspect of American culture – the jazz music which emanated from these poorer neighbourhoods. During an earlier visit, Veronica was compelled by what she describes as the "fantasy of the place", creating a series of vibrant reportage drawings effusing what she describes as the "romance of the architecture and city", pieces whose dynamic is typical of her more commercial practice.

This later piece of reportage, *Ninth Ward of New Orleans*, is equally evocative, although in stark contrast its mood is dense and static. The drawing documents a fleeting moment when a representative from a utility company painted a mark on the side of the building to symbolise its status – *not connected*. There is little remarkable or dramatic in this event: it is without the excited frenzy of earlier drawings of the Tour de France or Macy's parades, and the drawing is accordingly quieter and descriptive in a more lyrical way. Veronica has created a simple impression of this specific time and place, using it to make a symbolic statement about the monumental scale of the devastation, and "the diaspora of a displaced community". She observes, "The urban neighbourhoods like the Ninth Ward of New Orleans are more than collections of buildings, they are the resting places for the collective memories of generations of people." The cultural history and heritage of the Ninth Ward is resonant in vacant buildings such as this, being symbolically no longer 'connected'. As well as its representation, the drawing of this building becomes a symbol of this history, a direct articulation of its complex narratives.

A reportage drawing is a product of both a visual and an emotive engagement. The empathy expressed here results from Veronica being uniquely immersed in the environment at that specific time. "It's not like photography. You have to be present – you can't just grab it and go. You become involved in a way that maybe other people don't, and you capture moments." Here her focus on the marks on the sides of the buildings was significant, as "they all mean different things, so it felt like these houses were saying so much. The houses felt like people. The buildings were like witnesses, still standing."

The motives for Veronica's drawing trip to New Orleans were personal rather than commercial – there was no client brief. This addresses an urge to witness a reality, bringing a humanity to the documentation and revealing this through drawing. In such expressive drawings she manifests the physicality afforded by the process itself. "You're touching the paper, so your emotions come through the tactility."

Veronica wanted to consider something forgotten and unreported, to create drawings to bring people's attention to the issues she witnessed in New Orleans. Drawing as an act of social commentary can make an immediate social impact and also endure historically. "I did receive some reaction and comments to my blog posting of this story and art, but this neighbourhood needs a lot of help. It's my hope that publication of the drawings in *Understanding Illustration* and elsewhere can generate more interest in resolving the lingering issues of the Ninth Ward in New Orleans."

Veronica Lawlor lives in New York City, USA.

Ninth Ward
Self-initiated project, 2011

New Orleans sketch
Self-initiated project, 2011

"The quotidian arrests me. I can see that clearly and find joy in that."

Maira Kalman
And The Pursuit of Happiness

n the course of creating *And The Pursuit of Happiness* Maira Kalman fell madly in love with Abraham Lincoln, American President from 1860 to 1865. Before undertaking the year-long commission from *The New York Times* to produce a monthly blog about American democracy, she was unaware that he stood 7ft tall in his top hat. "I knew nothing about history and wasn't interested in politics." She endorses the notion of the artist or writer as an innocent, without an agenda, imagination fuelled by and not restrained by the "facts" of history. At the outset, she recalls, "I didn't know what I wanted to say or do. I knew I could bring a sense of naïveté but also a sense of curiosity to the project."

The first election of Barack Obama as President of the USA marked a significant historical moment, a time of global hope and optimism. That spirit was a catalyst and it fuelled this assignment. "It was a moment to look at this extraordinary country and get a glimpse of the extraordinary people who created it."

A restraining commission can also liberate, and Maira relishes the constraints, which she says, "allow me to create my own world". In this brief she travelled across America, her adopted country, to places she wouldn't usually visit, interrogating its past and reporting back affectionately on her experience and findings. This brief endorses the notion that fact and information can be creatively liberating, and Maira reflects, "To be sent on an assignment and bring back the story to tell you in image and text. *That* is fantastic freedom."

This democracy chronicle fuses fragments of information with observations and musings to present a circuitous yet linear set of images and words. She defines her work as being "journalistic", recording her experiences candidly. "I am less and less interested in my imagination and more interested in the real world. I love learning the true story."

The visual impression is of snapshots that document realities – the stylisation implies strongly that truth is interpreted by individual intervention. In these images there is a visual marriage of image and text. Maira's calligraphic sentences become an extension of the imagery, or vice versa. In terms of the relative function of these components she reveals, "the text and image support each other in very kind ways. My painting is narrative and my writing is illustrative".

Within this seamless patchwork there is no imposition of hierarchical importance within the content. The often banal subjects of everyday life are elevated and interwoven across a shared history to make them equal in status. No distinction is made between the historical facts garnered from the Lincoln archive in Philadelphia and the descriptions of the 'specials' on the menu at the Lincoln diner. This juxtaposition highlights connections between the past and the present as experienced by Maira.

The result is a funny, poignant narrative, seemingly random but carefully crafted. "There is an arc to each

And The Pursuit of Happiness
Client: *The New York Times*, January–December 2009.
Published by Penguin Press, a member of Penguin Group (USA), 2010

story, one thing does lead to another", which makes for a history that we can more readily connect with. "I go on tangents, digress, ruminate and doubt, and I know that there is an essential humanism that is conveyed."

The meanings are multifarious. It could be interpreted that great things are experienced through the ordinariness of our lives, or maybe that the lives of the great parallel our own. In essence, these images serve as a prompt for us to be conscious of the tangible evidence of the history which surrounds us, as well as recognising the stories created through our own existence. This demonstrates the power of illustration to connect empathetically with its audience.

In 1776, Thomas Jefferson momentously changed the words 'Life, liberty and the pursuit of property', in the Declaration of Independence to 'Life, liberty and the pursuit of happiness'. Maira Kalman has, through these images, put her own distinctive and indelible interpretative mark on American history. They have been compiled into a book format, and her vivid storytelling, far removed from arid, anonymous textbook history is now used in the USA to teach history to school children as young as 12 years old.

Maira Kalman was born in Israel and was raised and still lives in New York City, USA.

And The Pursuit of Happiness
Client: The New York Times, January–December 2009.
Published by Penguin Press, a member of Penguin Group (USA), 2010

The ANGeLs
aRe SiNgiNG
on this
gLoRious Day.

4

And The Pursuit of Happiness
Client: The New York Times, January–December 2009.
Published by Penguin Press, a member of Penguin Group (USA), 2010

on that BATTLEFIELD, LINCOLN gAVE ONE of history's gREAtEST SPEECHES, 272 WORDS Ending with

"government of the PEOPLE, by the PEOPLE, FOR the PEOPLE, shALL NOT PERISH FROM THIS EARTH."

WE ARE OVERWHELMED. WE NEED SOMETHING TO EAT.

70

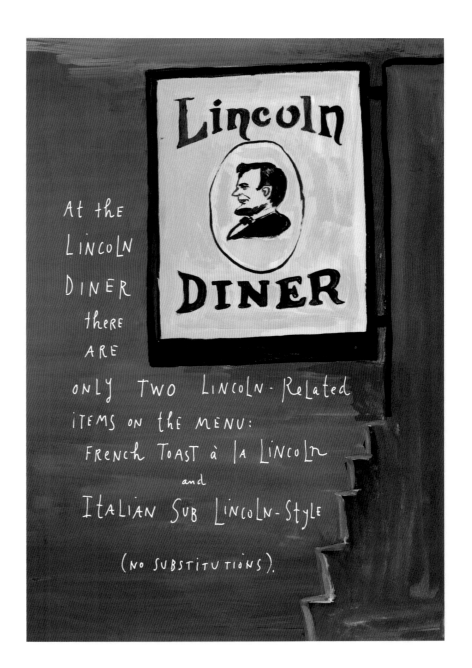

"You discover stories. It's uncomfortable."

Christopher Corr
The Mandarins

((t's like directing a film," says Christopher Corr, reflecting upon how he approaches commissions such as this one, namely, to illustrate *The Mandarins* by Simone de Beauvoir, for The Folio Society. "I think of the setting, and the characters and how best to place them within that location." In this case the choice of environments, their architecture and ambience has been informed by time spent travelling extensively across the world, drawing in situ. This particular book makes references to Lisbon, Guatemala, the USA and rural France – all places where he has drawn.

The stylisation in Christopher's work is a reminder that documenting a place as an illustrator isn't necessarily a quest for naturalistic or objective representation. Neither is his intention one of immediate commercial gain. "I like making pictures for somebody, but also I do pictures for me, and so through travelling to places I really want to go to," he explains, "I'm making pictures that lead to the commercial work." Christopher profits in other ways from the experience. "Travelling is so stimulating for my work. Working on location puts you into a different gear, makes you think faster, gives a sense of purpose."

The Mandarins by Simone de Beauvoir.
Published by The Folio Society, 2008.
Far left: cover and spine. Left: interior image

From a cursory glance the distinctions between location and commissioned work, such as these images, created in the studio in London, are undetectable. The circumstances for the location-based work are often physically challenging and unpredictable, and his reaction to them becomes a part of the fabric of the piece. This is something that he seeks to replicate in his commissioned pieces. "There are no battles in my studio. I have to work to create the tensions I want, the immediacy, vitality and energy."

Although Christopher says that he uses his own memories to inform the commissioned pieces, he often also refers directly to images drawn on previous trips. These pieces are evidence of a vital connection between his personal experience of the world through drawing on location and collaboration with an author to reveal new realities. The "truth" of the place as he has experienced it underpins his interpretation of the fiction written around the location. "I work alongside the author, I don't take a back seat. I aim to create, in a visual way, the sense of emotions."

In setting the scenes for the story, when describing both events and characters, Christopher evokes the atmosphere of the era (in this case the 1940s) as well as the location. The use of texture and pattern reflects cultural conventions specific to each place he describes, chronologically and physically. "Everywhere has its own particular character, its own look and feel. That's what I try and depict. I'm always looking for those details and characteristics that define a place."

His own sense of place is supplemented by research based on the specifics of the story. "It's important to show the correct character of a place. In general I show people of all types in my work, a good mix of male and female too." The detail is provided by reference to fashions and hairstyles from the time.

The boundaries of reality and fiction are not as distinct as the different activities of location drawing and illustration may imply. "I'm inventing all the time. Even on the street I don't see myself as a camera. I'm selective and choose how to arrange things."

As the life of the writer Simone de Beauvoir is reflected in the text, so Christopher's illustration is also biographical. Location drawing is a process of sensory and emotional experience as well as visual discovery, and the visual language used here is evidence of that. The cover image evokes the author's melancholy as expressed through the narrative. It is not specifically a depiction of postwar Paris but is suggestive of it – infused with the sense of the bleakness of those colourless times. It shows how it would feel rather than how it would look. Emotionally charged images befitting such a text are achieved largely through careful and selective use of what he refers to as the "language of colour", something Christopher describes as "the most powerful thing. We react instinctively to it – we feel it."

These images add to the written narrative, gaining much of their significance when 'read' alongside it. They embody the experiences and consequent stories of two separate artists, brought together for the commission, relying upon the visual literacy, emotional knowledge and subjective intervention of the viewer to make them real.

Christopher Corr works and lives in London, UK.

The Mandarins by Simone de Beauvoir

The Mandarins by Simone de Beauvoir. Location and
narrative-based commissioned work

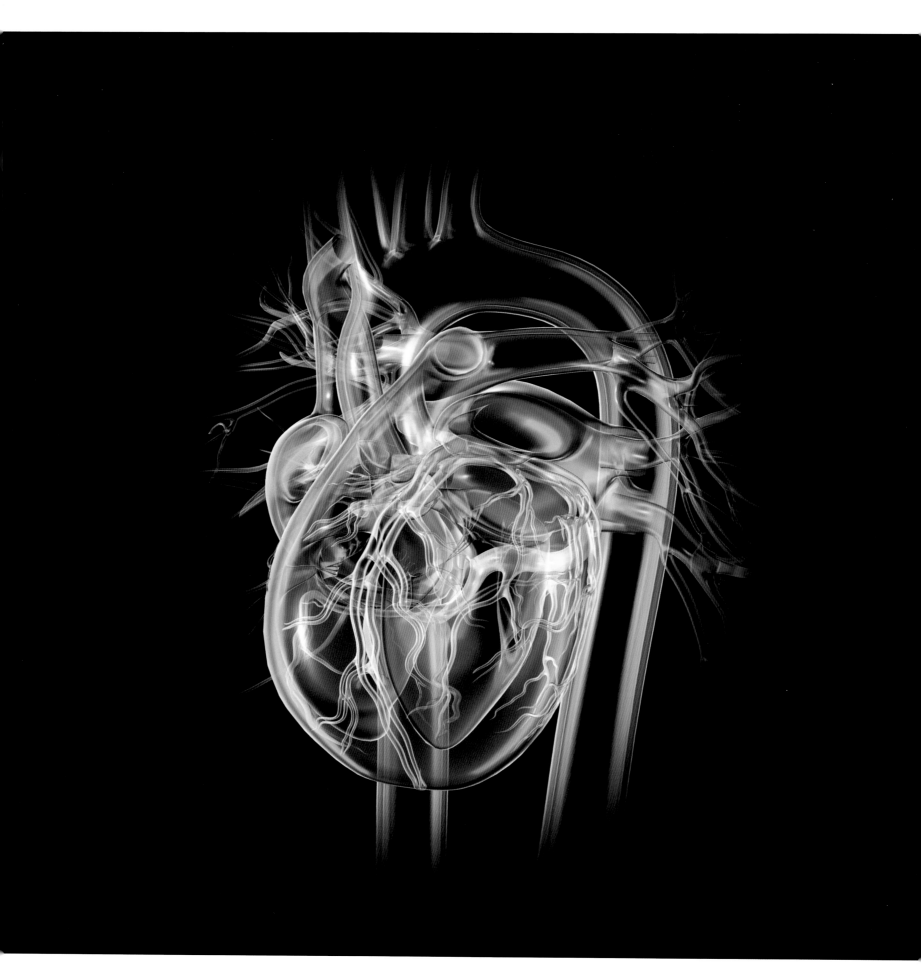

Craig Foster
Scientific and Medical illustration

Most of Craig Foster's work is esoteric in function, designed specifically for a medical rather than a lay audience. His work is often seen at trade shows, or is used by drug representatives, to demonstrate how a drug will work within the body or to describe how a new medical device functions. His illustrations represent and visualise complex medical information. "I'm most concerned with telling a scientific story. I want people to understand *how* science happens. My images are a simple way to gain conceptual understanding."

These images, taken as static frames composited from 3D animations, are typical of two definite genres within the niche area of medical illustration, each representing a different dimension of the field and each serving a very particular function. The scope for depiction has broadened rapidly, in line with gains in scientific understanding. It has evolved from classical description of the body on an anatomical level (as seen in the image of a heart, based usually on knowledge gained from dissection) to a more imaginative interpretation, the result of technological advances that have facilitated investigation at a deeper level to reveal atomic or molecular structures, such as the RAS cell representing the way protein pathways are structured within a cell. "What has changed today is that we can visualise proteins and molecular interaction in the same way we were able to visualise gross anatomy in the past."

His work contributes to advancements in science, and adds to the evolving medical knowledge base, the images giving visual form to information that has never been seen before. "I may get core information from a researcher or key expert, and then will do my own research too. There's usually some key bit of information that's not available or not published. Often times the mechanisms aren't fully understood and I will need to make an educated guess about how something works in order to develop the story."

The realm of practice in medical illustration has broadened thanks also to material advances within the corresponding field of art and design, and this is evident in the stylistic approaches seen here. Craig recalls, "When I first began pursuing a career in medical illustration, I thought I'd be in a hospital working for physicians or illustrating textbooks, doing a lot of pen and ink drawings, but the industry has changed, publishing has changed, and computers have changed the way we produce artwork. Almost all of my work is developed digitally."

Glass Heart
Self-promotional image. Create a unique transparent treatment of the heart to allow visualisation of the full coronary vasculature. The coronary artery is tinted red. The coronary vein is tinted blue.
Foster Medical Visualization, Inc. 2003

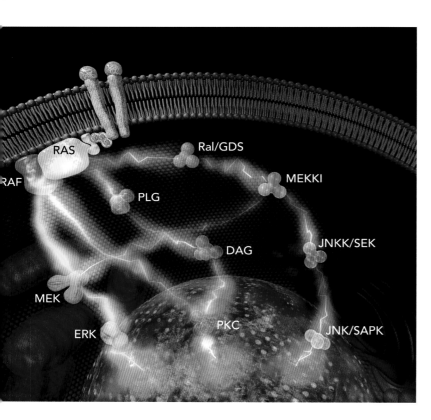

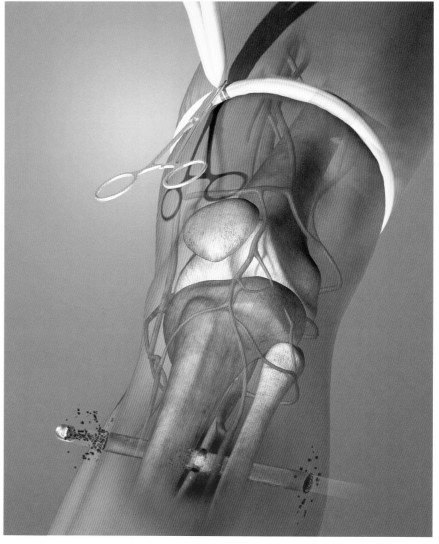

RAS cell

Image to explain how the RAF – MEK – ERK protein pathway fits into the broad chain of proteins within the cell that communicate between the cell surface and the nucleus. The pathway contains many proteins that act as an "on" or "off" switch. Control of these "on" or "off" proteins are being investigated as a possible cancer treatment. Client: Bayer Oncology / Onyx Pharmaceuticals, 2004

Tourniquet

Image to show treatment of a small calibre wound to the lower leg with a tourniquet. The wound (the damaged artery) is hard to control because the bullet entry is below the knee and hit the artery which was "protected" between the tibia and the fibula. The wound is difficult to compress from the exterior to halt the bleeding, thus the need for the tourniquet above the knee area. Published in the Journal of *Emergency Medical Services,* 2008

"I'm fascinated by the idea that our bodies are made of engineered molecular components. How these components come together to form a complex and functioning unit is truly amazing."

Craig's work is a synthesis of both art and science. "My knowledge base, derived from medical school courses, allows me to focus on the story and the aesthetics of an illustration as opposed to spending my time trying to grasp the science behind a project." Visual decisions are equal in significance to this scientific understanding, acquired over many years through study of cadavers during the medical thread of training and ongoing reference to medical diagrams and textbook drawings. "I tend to fall back on my fine-art background for my colour choices and design decisions. I use colour to guide the viewer based on what information needs to be prominent or what information needs to recede. My colour and design decisions help enhance recognition and understanding and make the story flow."

Some aspects of image-making traditionally considered to be creative are dictated by the nature of the information he is given. The visual conventions in this area of illustration have developed over time into a standard pictorial code – for instance, standard uses of colour. Veins are almost always shown to be blue, arteries red, and nerves yellow, as seen in *Tourniquet*, that shows the anatomical drawing of a knee. Referring to the protein image *RAS cell*, where he worked at a molecular level with information never described before, he says, "There is greater leeway for aesthetics in these new areas of study." He is inventing the language even as he uses it, describing and embodying visual information through new forms of expression.

"Science hasn't completely dictated how things should look on a cellular or microscopic level so there's more freedom to be creative. Current changes in technology are influencing visual choices and I'm starting to see more conventions in the way cellular components are represented."

His aims are both technical and creative – to give complex information the most appropriate visual form. "I'm often explaining how a particular mechanism operates within the body, and my focus is on telling the best story – to give better understanding and set up a visual flow through the illustration." When removed from their specific functional context the images can also be perceived subjectively, on a purely aesthetic level, and these visual properties are important to Craig. "I think about the fine art aspect of what I do all the time. If there's no audio or text the animations could be seen as pieces of art. I could see some of my drawings becoming sculptural pieces."

The exacting nature of the content requires accuracy and control in order to realise the story, but the images, although objective, are not clinical – they have personality and life. "Technically and aesthetically my work addresses ideas of structure and space. I'm motivated by the wonderment of how billions of tiny structures unite and interact to form us."

Craig Foster lives in the USA.

Incident in the Battle of Hastings (Gorby Hall programme)
Drawn on location for *Time Team*, 2010.
TV programme for Channel 4, UK

"Everything has to be correct, I'm very conscious of that, but that does not stop me drawing with my imagination."

Victor Ambrus
The Battle of Hastings

The work of Victor Ambrus exists at an intersection of art and science, embodying several forms of knowledge. This image, depicting an incident in The Battle of Hastings typifies the best of historical illustration, a genre that has characterised his long career: dynamic representation of an event, convincing in its visual detail and powerful in evoking the mood and drama associated with the action. The image was produced during his work for the archaeological excavation television programme *Time Team*. Victor's role here, as part of a team of archaeological and medical specialists, entails working reactively, for three days, on site within an excavation, bringing to life new discoveries literally as they are being unearthed. He visualises the knowledge embedded within the finds through the illustrations he creates, in circumstances and environments he describes as "demanding technically and professionally".

Such illustration should be considered as a form of documentation and realisation but also as a synthesis of both real and imagined events. "I make no distinction. They are digging up incredible real-life stories. I'm surprised by the amount of drama in there." The pieces exist also as documentation of the excavation process and of Victor's experience as an artist subconsciously reacting to the various forces shaping the experience, such as the weather and the nature of the stories uncovered.

This work requires exactitude: Victor is given a tight brief and embracing the constraints and specificity of the content that he deals with is integral to his methodology. His process dispels any myths of the stereotypical insular illustrator and proves the imperative for illustrators to work collaboratively. "I work hand in hand with science: pathologists, burns specialists, experts on the decay of the human form. I harass them, pump them for information." This information is the key to both visualisation and creating a narrative. "The advice I get about the skeleton reveals the sex and condition of the person and how they died, but also how they lived."

The Time Team can rapidly visualise buildings digitally, "but they can't conjure up figures". In these images they are convincing in their pose and gestures, and are also sensate. This is not academic drawing, but nonetheless it is a manner of representation that convinces the audience that the story is real, that the event happened. It is economical and edited with a sophisticated visual fluency and confidence underpinned by decades of studying the human form and by Victor's ability, accrued through illustrating over 300 historical books, to recall historical information. He reveals that, "Life drawing is very important to me. I'm always taking stuff out of my visual memory. I have to put something back." The credibility of the figures in this work is vital to its conviction.

The exacting nature of the content of historical illustration and factual constraints isn't inhibiting to the creative process. As Victor stresses, "Everything has to be correct, I'm very conscious of that, but that does not stop me drawing with my imagination."

These images vividly realise the stories contained within grey fragments of earth and bone, convincing us of the reality of the events depicted, but it is a human interpretation. The process Victor undertakes is often emotionally and physically challenging, influenced by revelations, "sometimes awful, shocking or sickening", such as the histories of dismembered corpses and victims of torture. He is conscious of his own emotional response and expresses empathy towards some of his subjects. Resonant in the depiction of battles is the latent impact of his own history in Hungary under siege by the Russians in the 1950s. "I was on the street when all hell let loose. It was traumatic, with people getting mowed down in front of me. I got out by the skin of my teeth. That's all part of my emotional background. I close my eyes and it's still there." He describes such experiences as "invaluable", and they infuse battle images such as this one with sincere sentiment.

Victor Ambrus is described as the illustrator who provides snapshots of history, but the effect here is more cinematic, like a still from an action movie. Accordingly, we can be enchanted, entertained and thrilled by the action he describes, but it's important to acknowledge also that such images have made a serious contribution to the popularisation of history, breathing life into the subject and also advancing academic knowledge.

Victor Ambrus, born László Győző Ambrus in Hungary, has lived in the UK since 1956.

Hanging Judge Jefferies
Display panel for Somerset County
Museum, The Castle, Taunton, 2009

Chariot Race, Colchester
Drawn on location for *Time Team*, 1998.
TV programme for Channel 4, UK

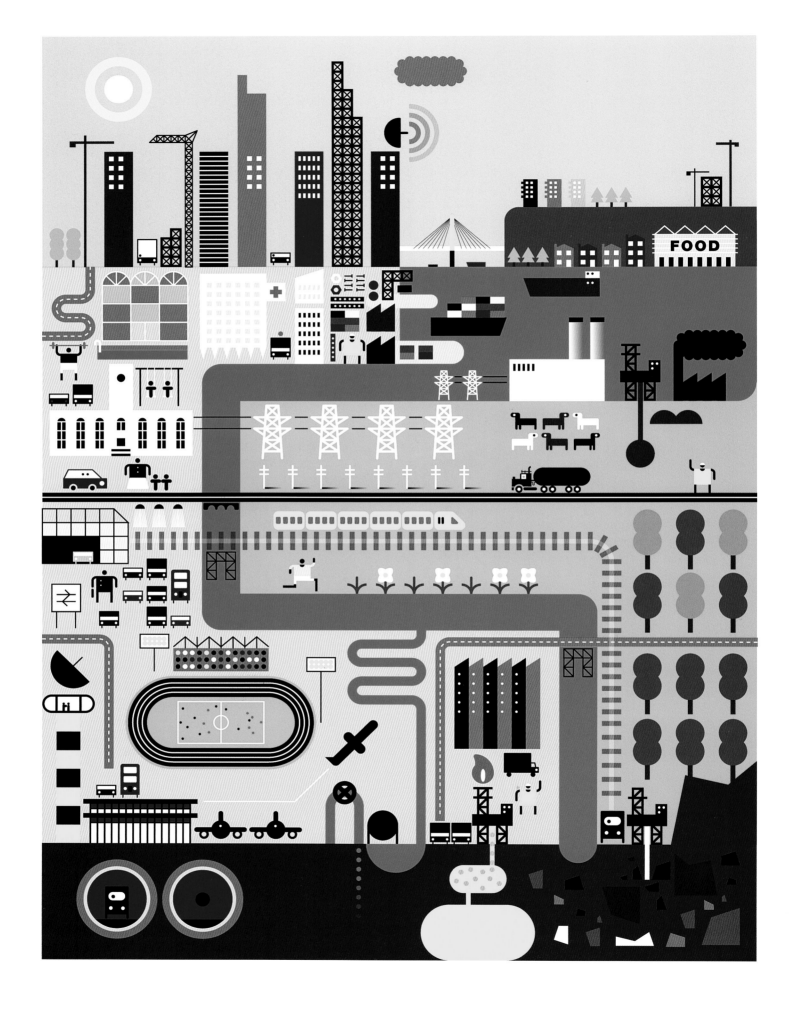

Peter Grundy
Laing poster

With its economical but sophisticated pictorial vocabulary this piece of information design, commissioned for Laing construction by the design group Black Sun, perfectly represents the work of Peter Grundy. He resolutely defines the function of his work as, "providing a solution for a problem", and in this case the brief was to express the various ways that Laing works within the environment, with the ensuing image intended for use within their corporate materials.

Complicated, prescribed information is effectively depicted here, without words and within a predetermined visual space. Constructed from a series of pictograms the image employs an icon-based visual system, typically defying conventions of viewpoint, scale and perspective, representing visual matter rather than depicting it. Peter elucidates: "The symbols are the actors, performing a role, turning information into concepts. They act to make people understand the meaning."

These components have their roots in the clean and elegant language of typography, his specialism as a student, and are reminiscent of universally recognised symbols as used within signage systems. Such elements have been developed and employed by Peter over his long career, not in pursuit of a coherent visual style, but as an expedient solution to design problems – to communicate a message. "The most important part of my images is the idea. People often see things in terms of style. I believe that a good idea can bring uninteresting data to life, but I think that's unlikely to happen with just style."

Such informational illustration employs a succinct visual shorthand. To convey the message with words rather than in a pictorial form could lack allure or impact, but this image has both of these qualities. It has the power to engage the audience both intellectually and aesthetically. Here a selective and carefully distributed palette, together with the repetition of shape across the picture plane, produces visual mnemonics which help the viewer retain the meaning. Using such classic design principles as these draws on an assumption that the audience shares a universally innate capacity to understand. Peter is conscious of this in that, "any elegance in the image isn't drawn – it's spatial. It uses eye skills that everyone has. That's the way one was taught design."

Laing Construction
An image to show the areas Laing operates in, in the form of a map/landscape. Client: Laing, commissioned by Black Sun, 2010

University of South Wales
Prifysgol De Cymru

Library Services

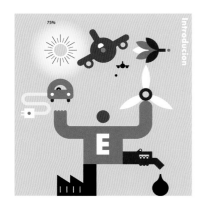

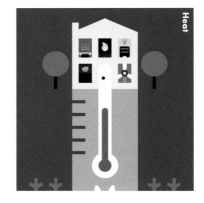

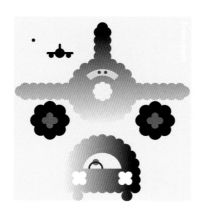

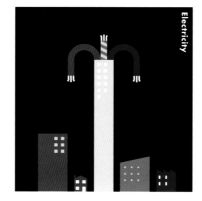

The Age of Energy
Client: Shell International and the *Telegraph* newspaper, 2010.
Weekly illustrations to accompany articles on energy issues.

"Having ideas about information, making complex things seem simple, that's the bedrock."

An image like this is a synthesis of intellectual and aesthetic content – the visual elements are vessels for meaning and the outcome is a language. Peter's education as a typographer and his knowledge of Swiss design has contributed to the evolution of both this language and the aesthetic sense within such pieces.

The way he organises elements spatially creates a visual hierarchy, ensuring that an image can be 'read' in the same way as a page of type. The style is incidental to this process and is something of which Peter is dismissive. He says, "Most people see the style first, but my primary objective is the idea. I have little control over the way my work looks. I can change the way I think about things but I have limited drawing capability. It's mechanical and simple because that's the way I draw – I work within my limits."

This image for Laing is complex and there is a sustainability built into it: Peter has factored future client needs into the design by building multiple scenarios into and throughout the piece. "Because I use simple ways to describe big business, these elements can be extracted and enlarged for other purposes in the future." Whilst this works as a one-off piece, Peter is known also for his involvement with clients and commissions – an involvement spanning decades – the cumulative effect of which is many interconnected images across many contexts for both screen and print. Often such bodies of work, like the expansive set of imagery produced for Shell International, reveal breadth within their range of communication, whilst sharing an identity: they are at once simple and complex. Peter reflects on how this is achieved. "What I seek is an idea, instantly communicating the message that will take the audience into the piece, inviting them to explore further." By taking very recognisable symbols and investing them with new meaning Peter injects humanity into the work. He explains, "The two main tools I use for this are humour and entertainment. The style isn't funny. The humour isn't in the drawing, it's in the idea of the drawing."

This can be a universal language – in such successful information design the viewer is capable of decoding signs and symbols and is able to interpret the meaning of the graphic content appropriately without the prop of words. The experience of Peter's images is a memorable one, allowing the messages included to endure.

Peter Grundy lives and works in the UK.

03 Message

Illustrators are able to present a view of events and issues that can clarify, illuminate or expand upon cultural content, as well as existing independently of context created by commissioners. It is a form of communication that can impart a direct or subtle message without the support of words.

These messages are expressed over a variety of platforms that can include a national and international forum through print and digital news media, independent publishing on the internet, or exhibition and portfolio production that may be part of a campaign or individual project. Organisations that wish to convey a message may utilise illustration, as will book publishers requiring the support of imagery to develop emotional complexity in a text.

Political illustration has an important role to play in critiquing and confronting those who wield power: it can reinforce the opinions and standpoints of the publication's readers, or challenge them with another view, potentially having the power to influence the viewer's opinion. Visual comment on public figures and politicians, often in the form of cartoons, has a long tradition in the press, and representations of those with influence can have social impact through caricature and satire.

Distillation of often complex ideas using symbols and metaphor to convey core elements is shown in the selection of political illustration. This simplification is the key preoccupation for Daniel Pudles and Edel Rodriguez in their artwork for national newspapers, using either black and white or a limited colour palette to allow the idea within the image to have maximum impact. Adopting a more authorial approach Steve Brodner has taken his individual and personal form of comment online using elements of video with verbal narration.

Such authorial projects based on a personally significant area or subject are initiated by artists, providing a voice outside the mainstream media, making these issues more visible through their depiction in illustrated imagery. Through reportage illustration of actual events such as the Gay Pride parade by Evan Turk, reflecting on all participants' perspectives, or Luba Lukova's *Social Justice* portfolio, which aims for a gut reaction from observers, an opportunity arises to change perceptions and increase empathy with the subject.

The campaigning organisation Ghosts of Gone Birds aims to increase support for endangered bird species through galvanising creative communities, and Edu Fuentes's triptych of extinct Hawaiian birds arises from a sympathy with the cause.

Illustrators can produce imagery with equal power for a number of different concerns if commissioned to do so, in the process revealing the way a visual language can be extended to encompass different requirements. But a passionately held belief is not a prerequisite to representing an issue effectively. Carlo Stanga and Serge Bloch work for clients across the industry but are able to concentrate their skills on the themes shown here – life-sustaining water, war, propaganda and peace – offering a universal resonance.

The architectural strengths of Carlo Stanga's work are combined with a symbolic approach in the piece for UNESCO that provided him with the opportunity to step beyond his usual visual realm. Contrastingly, Serge Bloch brings a distilled approach to the tale of *The Enemy*, while including a personal element to expand its universal theme.

As with the subjects addressed above, many issues benefit from a unique manner of presentation to an audience. Illness and death can be hard to confront, and tackling a child's fear of a parent dying requires an empathetic approach. Jim Kay's emotive illustrations for *A Monster Calls* by author Patrick Ness show the powerful connections that can exist between text and image, creating an atmosphere of menace whilst leaving space for the reader to identify with the story.

The work examined in this section testifies to the ongoing strength of illustration as both a cultural and social force. Whether working to commission or authorially, practitioners fulfil a vital role in educating, informing and influencing public opinion on the big issues of their time.

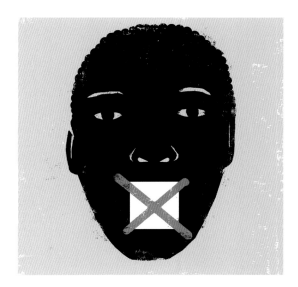

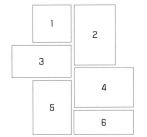

The enemy is over there but I have never seen him.
Every morning, I shoot at him. Then he shoots at me.

We both stay hidden the rest of the day, waiting.

1 **Edel Rodriguez**
  Voter Suppression

2 **Evan Turk**
  Seattle Gay Pride parade

3 **Steven Brodner**
  Biosphere Congress

4 **Serge Bloch**
  The Enemy

5 **Luba Lukova**
  Chernobyl, Fukushima...

6 **Jim Kay**
  A Monster Calls

Daniel Pudles
Nuclear Power and the Greens editorial

Sharp angles, grainy textures and a bold, minimal colour palette can make some of Daniel Pudles's woodcut editorial illustrations appear almost confrontational. Their striking shapes and attitude convey a keenness to tell a story without extraneous detail – but with a strong element of irony.

He covers a variety of areas for several publications, including book reviews for *The Economist* magazine and current affairs in *The Guardian* newspaper. These will have different approaches, where "I'm more aggressive, maybe, in the way I approach the picture. I'm more ironic or sneering when I draw for *The Guardian*, for example." This image, created for George Monbiot's weekly environmental column, illustrates the journalist's comments on the view of former and current Friends of the Earth directors who suggested the UK Prime Minister abandon new nuclear power stations. Daniel represents the columnist's opinion that not all power needs can be replaced with alternative forms of energy, that this view is short-sighted. "We do not possess an abundance of good choices, and cannot afford to start throwing options away," states Monbiot.

While attacking nuclear strategies, the 'Green' leaf is blinkering the character, preventing him seeing that there may be alternatives to his own viewpoint, while Death lurks in the background. The exaggerated expressions reveal the humour below the serious subject matter. "With my illustrations I think rhythmically," Daniel comments, "It goes bing, bang, boo. There are often three elements in my illustrations, I realised, so I often work with trinities – an uneven number of elements." The wood grain and carefully placed, but deliberately mis-registered, colours contribute to a sense of rawness in the image – almost anti-slickness – which emphasises the heightened emotions depicted.

His artwork comments on the human condition, whether it be intolerance, greed or indifference to others' suffering, "It's this thing with humanity; I think we're all slightly ridiculous, really. Maybe that's my view on human animals. I don't want to be kind to ourselves. We are illogical; we think we are gods, but we're just animals."

The brief will sometimes be received as the full copy but often, with tight editorial deadlines, the piece is a work in progress, and so illustrator and writer will speak over the telephone, allowing Daniel to pick up the general tone and personal direction of the piece. "It's better coming from the writer than the art director, because from the art director it can be pretty dry." Ideas for the image form as he's talking to the writer and he will then start drawing them. "Mostly they work, and then I rework them slightly, because when you draw it changes what you had in your mind." It's a bonus if the writer appreciates the image concept, but ultimately it is the editor who approves the idea.

Every element in an image is important, with ideas pared down to form a simple composition and unnecessary detail excluded. "If a guy doesn't need an arm or his eye," he laughs, "I gouge them out!" He considers that small details, such as realistic clothing, distract the viewer's eye away from the main idea, which he does not always present in an easily digestible manner. "I'm never lazy when it comes to looking for an idea. I try to avoid the easy solutions, to make it too soft. I need some grit, really. That keeps me interested as well." However, images for *The Economist* book reviews have a lighter, more distanced approach, as they are serving a less direct purpose.

Greens and nuclear power
For George Monbiot's Comment page. Article about former directors of Friends of the Earth who had written to the UK Prime Minister suggesting he abandons new nuclear plants, *The Guardian*, 2012

In the past artwork was created using mixed media, but woodcut is now his preferred method, though Daniel acknowledges he is not a great technician. "Woodcut conveys my ideas much more directly and simply as well. It's just a technique I use, but I'm not precious about that technique." Prints are then scanned and coloured digitally, freeing him from the time-consuming process of cutting additional blocks for colours. Some of these works are animated by Daniel, a challenge he has set himself, and *The Guardian* images lend themselves well to the creation of a story. "In animation everything is in rhythm and details ... to see it all work, it's really magical."

As an editorial illustrator he believes it's important to have a connection with the culture he is commenting on. Although born in Paris, he now resides in Brussels, but having spent many years living in the UK he has a strong affinity with the country – "There's a chemistry between the UK and me" – and feels that commissions from other European countries do not always bring the same excitement a British brief can generate, "In the UK you have top journalists, brilliant writers – they can write about dry subjects in a very passionate and interesting way." Those writers have a dynamic foil in Daniel Pudles.

Daniel Pudles lives in Belgium.

For an article on an actor in Shakespeare's time who acted on Sundays when he should have been attending church. A bishop condemned him and he was imprisoned in stocks and made to wear a donkey's ears. Writer: Dr Martin Wiggins, *Around The Globe magazine*, 2012

"The copy can be quite serious
and dramatic, but I always try
to get some irony in there."

'Hey babe, take a walk on the wild side'
Review of Haruki Murakami's novel, *1Q84*, *The Economist*, 2011

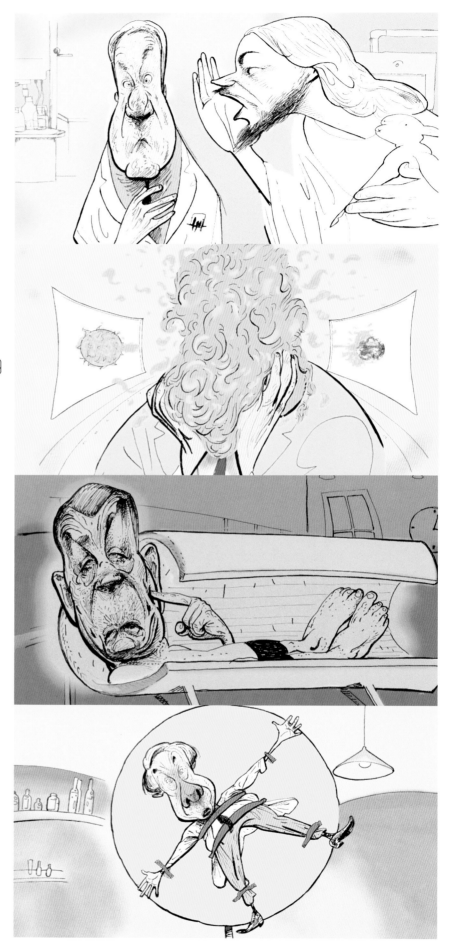

"It's all about communicating clearly with strangers."

Smashing Crayons/Biosphere Congress – self-initiated project based on *Need to Know* series for American TV station, TVS, 2012. Written and illustrated by Steven Brodner. View the video: http://player.vimeo.com/video/24419407

Steve Brodner
Biosphere Congress film

n a media-driven world which bombards us with ephemeral images, reporting news as it breaks, the satirical art of Steve Brodner offers enduring opportunities for reflection – an overt and individual perspective on politics. Although for more than three decades his "journalistic art" has addressed the diverse issues that define our times, he reflects, "There's really only one big issue, and it's the intersection of politics and money: democracy has been purchased by extremely wealthy people." His visual response results in sometimes controversial images, often involving caricatures of political and cultural figures. His message is genuinely personal, "Our social issues, such as debt crisis and financial deprivation, global warming, health care, don't matter to the people with power because it's all fine for them. I try to give an honest take on how I feel about such things."

He adopts a largely authorial position, approaching the pool of clients – magazines and newspapers with whom there is empathy – so that many of his assignments are self-generated. These compelling images exist alongside text in an editorial, print-based environment, though he also creates images specifically for the screen.

The film featured here represents an extension, authorially, of the assignment he did for the *Need to Know* series for American TV station TVS. Whereas that assignment entailed collaboration with directors, editors, sound men and production specialists, in films such as *Biosphere Congress*, where he considers political attitudes towards global warming, he takes sole responsibility for all aspects of the communication process: conceptual, creative and technical. In the video it is Steve we hear narrating his own researched script. This process of learning how to work in a relatively new format is something he describes as "like building a plane as it's taking off".

Whether the artwork is a static image or part of a film such as this, it gains its value through the content. Steve quotes the eminent late designer, Paul Rand, when he says, "Art is what happens when an idea finds its perfect form." In the design process the idea follows the problem, and Paul sees that it is visual communication, the process of problem solving, that is the thrust of his work. "How can you be a cartoonist and try to be entertaining and say one true thing, while negotiating a highly complex issue is the problem we have to negotiate. My solution is if I can say only one true thing, let me do that in a powerful way and open up thought, inquisition and observation by the viewer to think about something that hadn't been considered." Of the form he says, "it must fit the ideas. It's about the context, the subject. I want to make it as clear as possible."

His messages are conveyed through irony – "saying *a* and meaning *b*" – and metaphor is often the vehicle for the ideas. As interpretation of metaphor is culturally biased, Steve can more confidently presume that the audience will be sufficiently well informed to understand his references when he works editorially for publications, as they have a recognised demographic. When illustrating for films such as this, gauging the audience is not clear-cut, and he acknowledges that what is successful in print may not be a good solution on video.

His metaphors make references to popular rather than high culture, to avoid making his imagery too exclusive, but Steve acknowledges that, "what it is in the metaphors that connect is always mysterious." He describes developing "the third eye", which allows him to distance himself, seeing a piece from an external

perspective. "I have to know how far I can go before I lose my perception and it becomes something else – it's easy to be misunderstood." He talks about the hierarchy of ideas, revealing, "often that means not going with your first idea, continuing to work until you get something that is layered, more complex, and invites further investigation by the reader or viewer."

Of the caricatures which feature in all dimensions of his work, here of politicians who will be recognised in the USA, Steve says, "People present an image. I *think* of them as symbols and images rather than human beings. I draw them the way that people think of them."

Although many images are coded and difficult to access fully by those outside the time or place for which they were intended, the ongoing relevance of many of the underlying issues gives Steve's art longevity, whether for print or screen-based work. They are also a potent reminder of the power of illustration to be both a social signifier and a social force. "Culture by consensus will decide which images are most gripping, salient and powerful – they become part of the national conversation."

Steve Brodner lives in the USA.

The Sound of Sarah
The New Yorker magazine, 2012

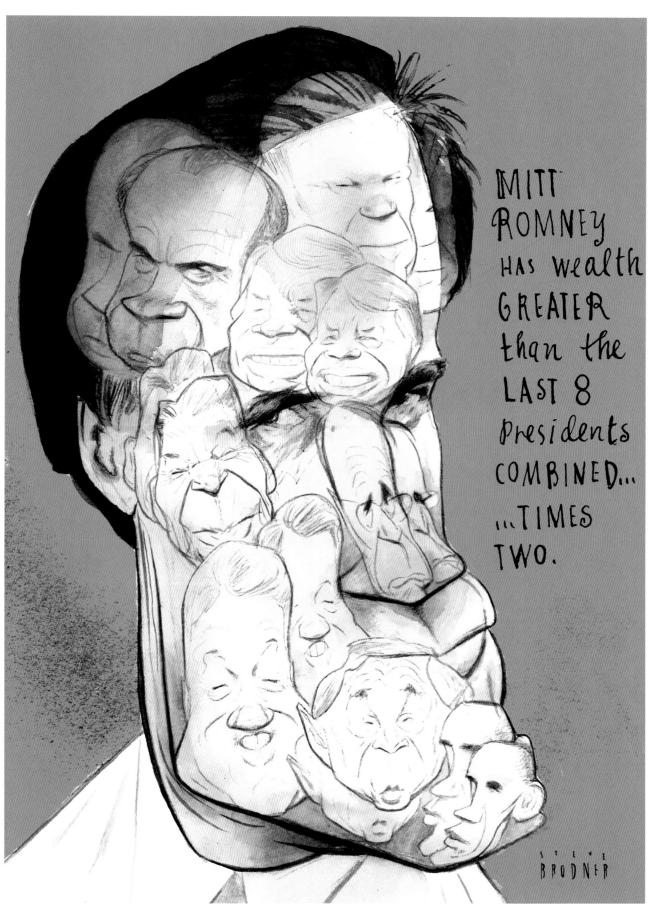

MITT ROMNEY HAS wealth GREATER than the LAST 8 Presidents COMBINED... ...TIMES TWO.

Mitt Romney is Richer than …
The American Prospect, 2012

A selection of images commissioned for publication
for *The Washington Spectator* in print and online
www.washingtonspectator.org

America leaves Iraq
The Washington Spectator, 2012
Raise The Minimum Wage
The Washington Spectator, 2012
How the CIA handles its whistle blowers
The Washington Spectator, 2012

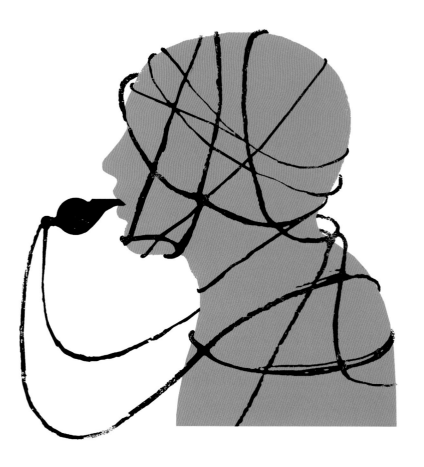

Edel Rodriguez
The Washington Spectator

Voter Suppression
The Washington Spectator, 2012

The strong iconic work Edel Rodriguez produces on a bi-weekly basis for *The Washington Spectator* is a form of visual communication that reveals the essential intellectual and conceptual power of the illustrator within the collaborative process of editorial, ideas-based illustration. Here there is an opportunity to make strong statements revealing an autonomy of the illustrator's opinion whatever the content supplied by the art editor. "The information from *The Washington Spectator* varies to a great degree," Edel says. "Sometimes I get a couple of sentences of information, sometimes the full, unedited article."

The themes underpinning politically reflective editorial work have resonance for the life of the illustrator as well as the life of the readers. "I've seen the repercussion of politics, the effects of societal forces like religion, seen families torn apart by emigration," he says, "Memory, nostalgia, identity, war, cultural displacement, and mortality are all themes I explore through my work."

At War
Book cover of **Girls At War and
Other Stories** by Chinua Achebe,
published by Anchor, 2010

"I think illustrators, artists and content creators in general have a big impact on society. It's hard to quantify an individual's imprint on society right now. But looking back through the prism of history, one can see how poster artists, designers, musicians, etc. have come together and impacted society for the better. I believe the job at hand is for all of us to do the best we can, and let history unfold."

The social conscience shaping this work, and a conviction in the power of imagery to be functional in influencing opinion and social action, has roots both in his personal connection with the issues explored and a recognition of the potential power of imagery to reach an audience. In Edel's early childhood, experienced during a dictatorship in his native Cuba where, "my friends and family were taken advantage of, abused, roughed up", he was surrounded by communist revolutionary images and posters, images of tanks, guns and revolutionary, nationalist, anti-American propaganda. When at nine years old he moved to the USA, he witnessed individual freedom from oppression and had the experience of social justice. This new life was coloured by the propaganda of capitalism in the form of advertising.

These experiences are synthesised, latently, in these illustrations. In a culture of increasing visual literacy, imagery is powerful and Edel optimises the potential to "sell an idea". "I was always interested in visuals, and these two cultures, communist and capitalist, clashed when I was a child. I think the combinations of the two cultures still shows up in my work to this day." In this regard, he is very principled, turning down commissions that run contrary to his own convictions.

These works reveal the potential for illustration to have an impact culturally as a subtle form of propaganda where impact can transcend the text

it is commissioned to accompany. Editorial pieces once considered ephemeral and as transient as news items are given longevity through publication and circulation outside their original defining context – through availability via the web and exhibitions in gallery spaces. Exceeding the potential of single fine-art pieces created for a gallery environment they reach a broad audience, often in excess of the 60,000 circulation of the periodical. Hence the work is perceived as a more general reflection of culture, politics and modern times rather than restricted to the meaning suggested by headlines in the editorial.

Whilst there is universal resonance in many of these images, when they are anchored to the article their message has specific connotations. Edel suggests that as a piece of illustration the image's marriage to the text reflects its function in the editorial context, revealing also how it will be consumed by an audience. "A good illustration works as a teaser to get the reader into the article. The full answer is found once the article is read and the reader makes the connection to the image." He reminds us of the important role of the art editor as the facilitator in this negotiation. "The editors understand that a good illustration has to be focused, so they get that not all the parts of the article are shown in the image."

The black and white aesthetic dictated by the commission results in a powerful symbolic directness, a

graphic quality that often compels visual engagement. "Form follows function, I suppose," Edel says, reflecting on the importance of this visual economy. He adds, "I like to follow through on ideas and see where they lead, and not get caught up in the trappings of 'style'." The visual language reflects a firm symbiosis between the aesthetic and the concept. "I've been able to integrate symbols and metaphors in a better way over time, I think. As one develops one's work, the graphics evolve to accommodate the ideas. Over time, there's a smoother flow, and give and take, between idea and execution."

Edel acknowledges the process of communication is complex and the audience's visual literacy is influenced by experiences other than his own as the artist. "I'm conscious that the image will be seen and processed by a viewer, so I make an effort to be clear about my intentions. However, the audience can be so varied and bring so much to the table themselves that there's a limit to what I can do. Sometimes I like hearing people's interpretations of my images. They can be so completely disconnected from my intentions, but I get a kick out of that." Whilst there is no absolute meaning within an image, there is value to the message. "It's the wonder of art, people can get so many things from it."

Edel Rodriguez was born in Cuba and lives in New York, USA.

Evan Turk
Seattle Gay Pride reportage

E van Turk created the *A Picture For A Thousand Voices* project to collect stories and create illustration for the gay rights movement, specifically to become an active participant. "I think that there is often a lack of illustration that speaks about gay experiences in personal and understandable ways, so I wanted to start collecting and creating work that brought a closer eye to that side of gay rights." Since starting the project, he has created reportage of various events related to gay rights in different American cities, including the 2011 Pride Parade in Seattle.

With this drawing of drag queens and muscle guys from the Seattle event Evan wanted to include the explosion of sights, sounds and colour that is part of a pride parade, but without presenting the characters as stereotypes. "One of the wonderful things about reportage for me is that, although I always try to include the 'archetypes' of a particular event, because they are a huge part of it, when you are on location these people are always individuals. With reportage, they are always real people that I saw and had a connection with, however brief, just by drawing them."

Seattle Gay Pride reportage
Participants in the Seattle Gay Pride parade
Self-initiated reportage project, 2011

Before attending an event Evan will sketch plans of various possible page layouts in thumbnail form to organise the event in his mind and decide what he needs effectively to cover it, even if it's just for personal work, such as with the gay pride drawings. "I like to think about different image shapes and layouts, so I will have a variety of different picture designs at the end of each event. It helps me to make some decisions beforehand, so that I can be more relaxed and draw more spontaneous things as they come as well." He may also read about the event and its history to assist in picking up on important symbols while there.

A fast-moving event such as this allows no time for second-guessing any decisions. "You just have to follow your gut and keep drawing, or otherwise the whole thing will pass you by. It makes for drawings with more spontaneity and energy. I probably had less than a minute to try and get the people in this image down on paper, since they were on a float driving quickly by." Rapid pencil lines and smears of colour add to the sense of movement, with the closeness of the figures giving a sensation of immersion in the event.

This inclusivity, showing the whole event, means that Evan expands the story by also turning his eye to those watching the march and celebrating equally the older people and possible first-timers sharing an empowering event such as this. "With gay pride, there is always the sense of fun, freedom and sexuality, but with this series I also wanted to show the side of gay pride that is more sensitive, moving and powerful, and that people might not think about as much. But those powerful moments

First day for gay marriage in the state of New York
City Clerk's office in Lower Manhattan, self-initiated reportage project, 2011

Lesbian biker, Seattle Gay Pride parade, 2011

occur within the context of a flamboyant parade with loud music, nudity and rainbow flags. It was important to me to capture both sides of the event, the humour and the feeling, because each one exists because of the other."

Portraying a sense of place, as well as the human activity, is important and each of those two elements contributes communication opportunities with the other. "The people bring the place to life with individuality, and the place grounds the people in the context and symbols of the environment."

This series, as a part of a larger body of work related to the gay rights movement, has been an interesting journey for Evan. As an under-represented subject within illustration, it is one that he plans to continue exploring. "It's a topic that keeps evolving, and my own work keeps evolving as I learn, so it's been exciting for me to see how my own drawings have changed." Such issues-based work can contribute to social change. He recognises that both his drawings and the gay rights scene have progressed from the first gay rights protest he drew in 2008 to the passing of marriage equality in New York in 2011.

He is optimistic about the place for reportage in illustration, here reporting on gay culture and potimising the potential of this to reach a broader audience. He believes people tend to have a fascination with seeing artists draw on location and with work created in that way. "I think that because it's always about responding to the moment, it will always remain relevant."

Evan Turk lives in the USA.

First day for gay marriage in the state of New York, Nancy and Yolanda, 2011

The line for marriage outside the City Clerk's office, 2011

social justice 2008   censorship

"About my interest in social issues and justice;
I believe that this is the purpose of art in
general. Art is always political."

Luba Lukova
Social Justice portfolio

Powerful, dynamic images that speak as bold statements make up Luba Lukova's Social Justice portfolio and her commissioned illustration work. Her images on health, race, corporate corruption, brainwashing and the income gap in society communicate through metaphor, consciously tackling subjects that are rarely faced by many commercial artists, encapsulating issues with deceptive simplicity. Many of her images, such as this one, are aiming for a visceral reaction. "I feel for the issues I depict and I always try to make the viewer react to my work. I believe this is the greatest power art has, to change perception and increase empathy."

This *Censorship* image initially appeared as a commissioned cover for the Art & Leisure section of the *Sunday New York Times* for a feature on how the Taliban regime in Afghanistan censored music. "The article described how the Taliban beat the musicians with their instruments. So I thought that an image with the flutist's fingers nailed to the flute would be a strong metaphor for the issue." Luba recalls the art director was concerned the editor might not like it, "since the paper normally doesn't want to disturb people while they're having coffee on Sunday morning. But the editor loved it and it was printed without any changes." Many of her clients approach her having seen her personal work, and share her ideas – "They trust me and give me freedom to deal with the assignments" – resulting in close connections between her commissioned illustrations and personal projects. This image was subsequently published as a poster in Luba's *Social Justice* portfolio, due to its relevance as a more general statement about censorship, "Because we experience censorship in the free world, too, and it is always painful when we are not allowed to express our thoughts in a free way."

In *Censorship* the selection of one bright colour effectively contrasts with the black and white, concentrating the image and allowing room for interpretation without diluting the message. Colours were chosen carefully to reinforce the impact of the image: "Red and black was the perfect combination to express the pain in the *Censorship* image."

The viewer is required to do some work when facing her images. "They need to complete my pictures in their heads, somehow to find the answers for themselves. I think the most effective art works that way – with metaphors, not with didactics." Bold black line and an intense, but limited, palette is a constant feature in Luba's images, giving them a strong impact as commissions and posters.

Censorship
Poster from "*Social Justice* 2008" poster portfolio, published by Clay & Gold, offset. The image was first published on the cover of the *Sunday New York Times,* Arts & Leisure section, 2008

Chernobyl, Fukushima …
Silk-screened poster commemorating the Chernobyl and Fukushima nuclear disasters. Commissioned by the Triennial of Eco Posters in Ukraine, 2011

Luba Lukova in the Delta
Exhibition poster for Lukova's show at Wright Gallery, Cleveland, MS, USA, lithograph, 2012

LUBA LUKOVA IN THE DELTA 2.2-29.2012 WRIGHT GALLERY
SOCIAL JUSTICE & OTHER WORKS DELTA STATE UNIVERSITY CLEVELAND, MS

Projects are approached differently; sometimes she will do a lot of research – "and I love that part because I'm a curious person" – other times ideas distil themselves speedily and few sketches need to be done. She believes it is important to be a clear thinker and have a good comprehension of the issues to visualise ideas. "To have a logic, but then twist that logic and present it in an unexpected way that surprises the viewer. I don't like to tell people what's right or wrong. I prefer to make them think and let them decide for themselves."

Luba believes that art is always political, "Even if you decide to paint only flowers, this is a political act because you refuse to deal with anything else," although motivation to communicate on injustice and social concerns comes partly from a personal area; if her own experience does not relate to the issue, she will contemplate how it would have made her feel should it have happened to her, and will use her imagination to express it as an image. "When I think about art from other genres that has affected me, like theatre or literature, it is always work that has dug deep into the most personal and social issues at the same time. These two categories are intertwined in good art. In my own work, I'm not able to come up with ideas if I don't care about a problem. In that sense, everything I do is personal."

The *Social Justice* portfolio is exhibited around the world, and it is also encouraging that Luba's artwork, although demanding, is used within the illustration marketplace. "I think we live in a time that needs challenging art more than ever, and that's good for the profession. Hopefully, visual art and illustration can provoke deeper thinking and understanding of the problems we face today."

Luba Lukova was born in Bulgaria and lives in the USA.

Lāna'i Hookbill
Ghosts of Gone Birds,
for exhibition, 2012

"I wanted to find the balance between the sad facts of extinction and a cute, appealing image."

Edu Fuentes
Ghosts of Gone Birds exhibition

Organisations supporting conservation need a way of drawing attention to their cause, and Ghosts of Gone Birds has done this by inviting artists, writers and performers to communicate the urgent message about bird species facing extinction through their chosen medium.

Ghosts of Gone Birds was conceived and is run by documentary film-maker and art collector Ceri Levy, and creative director Chris Aldhous of ideas agency Good Pilot, with the aim to raise funds for the Bird Life Preventing Extinctions Programme through sales of artwork and donations from visitors to the project's exhibitions. These have been held at various events and venues throughout the UK, from 2011 onwards, and are forming a new way for people to connect with conservation.

Edu Fuentes was invited to participate by Good Pilot after attending a Ghosts of Gone Birds exhibition in London. He had not been aware that there were so many extinct bird species "When I was given the full 20-page document full of bird names I was shocked!" He recognised that it was a positive move to be involved. "It's good to know there are people out there trying to stop this."

The goal of images created for the Ghosts of Gone Birds project is to raise money, and these are sold framed or as unframed prints from the gallery shows. "My aim was to create beautiful images that people would look at and think, "I'd like to have that in my living room," confirms Edu. "I wanted to find the balance between the sad facts of extinction and a cute, appealing image." It is a simple concept, but the positive reaction triggered by the beauty of the birds in the images emphasises the fact that these creatures actually no longer exist, and life for many other bird species is precarious, hopefully prompting an interest from the public in supporting the conservation work being undertaken to protect them – here illustration is acting as a catalyst for change.

Although finding the list overwhelming, the birds Edu eventually chose to make images of were Hawaiian: the Kākāwahie, a type of finch, the Bishop's 'O'o and the Lāna'i hookbill. He was attracted to these because of their pleasing shapes and colourful plumage, saying, "I thought I'd enjoy translating the quirkiness of their feathers to my visual language." In spite of the birds being extinct, Edo found enough reference images on the internet to give him a good sense of their physiognomies, mostly through old zoology drawings and etchings.

Telling the wider part of each bird's story was an important element in creating the images. "Apart from the beauty of the birds, I also wanted to show their habitats and the reasons for their extinction. They're all there: predation by cats and rats, the pineapple palm-tree plantations that destroyed their forests, grazing animals and mosquitoes carrying disease." Edu depicts these elements in deftly composed images giving clear clues as to the birds' demise, but retaining an overall appeal, something illustration can successfully achieve – giving issue-based work a broader impact. The environments surrounding the birds were also researched. "But", he adds, "I took some artistic licence too!" Time was spent to achieve the right colour schemes, and once the basic palette was decided on he tried out different combinations for the bird's plumage. "Sometimes you stick with the first one, sometimes a new, unexpected combination emerges. This 'controlled randomness' is vital for having fun and for creating something not too rational, something that breathes." Although created mainly in Illustrator, the addition of texture, grain and scratches in Photoshop contributes to the appeal of the images. "This step is important to me, as I like to find a balance between the perfect geometry of vectors and the warm, handmade feel of textures."

Edu's participation in the broader illustration world extends to the formation of the *Happy Wednesday* webzine with two colleagues, which started as an online showcase but "became our experimenting lab for all the things we couldn't (or didn't have time to) do in our daily work, from animation to 3D to even designing HTML-based mini-video games!" Other artists now also contribute. "We think this interchange of ideas is very refreshing, and social media is allowing us to contact all kinds of artists internationally."

This reaching out to a wider audience chimes with the philosophy of Ghosts of Gone Birds, exploiting the primary function of illustration to act as a tool of communication, and in this case as a call to action to save more bird species from extinction.

Edu Fuentes was born in Spain and now lives in the UK.

The Bishop's 'O'o
For the exhibition Ghosts
of Gone Birds, 2012

Kākāwahie
For the exhibition Ghosts
of Gone Birds, 2012

The Enemy
(Cover, Australian edition),
written by Davide Cali, illustrated
by Serge Bloch, 2010

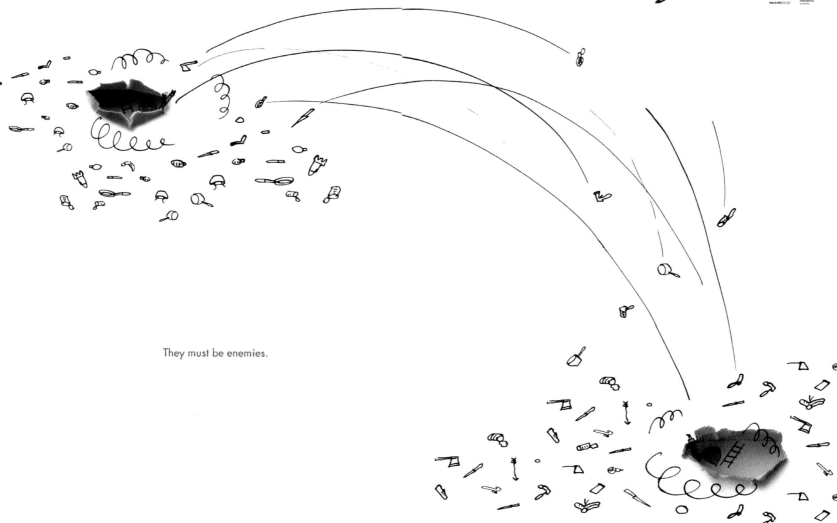

They must be enemies.

"I come from Alsace near the German border – a strange place for peace and war. As I'm Jewish, all this has another dimension."

Serge Bloch
The Enemy: A Book about Peace

As conflict and war continue to be destructive forces, *The Enemy*, written by Davide Cali and illustrated by Serge Bloch has an optimistic message as a book about peace. We are asked, 'Look, do you see two holes?' On each side of the spread a photograph of a hole, a rip in the paper. Over subsequent spreads we learn that in each hole there is a soldier and that they are enemies, and then the fable begins.

In the early spreads of the book, one soldier's monologue is delivered through simple text, usually positioned at the base of the page, married with the illustrator's minimal drawings. An inexact symmetry is created, with one page often mirroring the other. The book as a format is a perfect vehicle for *The Enemy* – two pages create opposite sides, the gutter creating a barrier between warring factions. Because the character barely moves, there is a sense of repetition that endorses the frustration expressed through the text. Resonant of *Endgame* by Samuel Beckett, the wait of the solitary character seems interminable and we begin to experience his sense of futility. The illustrator engineers this theatricality in the piece. "I wanted to transform the book," says Serge. "I made it into a stage." In doing so he compels us to engage as an audience with the drama, suspending our disbelief.

The bleakness of the situation is reiterated by the desert-like sparseness of each page. Serge's distilled drawings; the scratchy black ink line and the khaki tones of watercolour that anchor the illustrations to the book's white pages are compelling. He reveals that working at other times in his career with American art directors who repeatedly seek images where, "less is more" has taught him how to create impact. "I use a simple style because the idea itself is very strong." Serge explains. "It's important to go directly to this idea so that the reader can go easily into the book."

The white space on the pages emphasises the sense of the character's isolation and mounting desolation within his unchanging situation. "We start to know the character," Serge explains. "The book is about hate: we see that you have to learn to hate the person to fight with him."

From his hole the soldier shoots at the enemy. Across time and seasons he crouches in his hole wondering about the enemy, who neither he nor we ever see. The design of the pages mirrors the evolution of the character's philosophical position, being unchanging in his hate then gaining an increased curiosity about the enemy, a transformation that symbolically culminates in him leaving his own hole. *'At last I reach the enemy's*

hole…' he says, *'there are pictures of his own family. I wasn't expecting him to have a family.'* Overleaf there are photographs of the illustrator as a child with his parents and siblings. These photographic images signify a transition from the soldier's false beliefs, which we learn were instilled as a result of propaganda, to the reality of the situation and an ensuing sense of compassion and understanding born from the realisation that the enemy is also a real person.

Serge considers his decision to move from his signature graphic drawing to include these actual elements at this point in the narrative. "It's important for me that it's a real family, to show they are human beings – the enemy is not a monster." In Serge's other illustration projects across many platforms and applications, including advertising and editorial, the use of photography with line achieves an aesthetic effect that has become his distinctive visual style. As he says, "The contrast of the graphic element and the strength of the line, that is my language."

This book provided the illustrator with a rare opportunity to work on a project where this use of photography has a deeper significance, linking as it does to his own family history. "I come from Alsace near the German border – a strange place for peace and war. As I'm

The Enemy
Written by Davide Cali and illustrated by Serge Bloch,
published by Schwartz & Wade, 2009

Sometimes I think the others have forgotten us. Maybe the war is over, and no one remembered to tell us.

Or maybe we are the last two soldiers fighting. Maybe whichever one of us survives will win the war.

At night, there are lots of stars above my hole. I wonder if the enemy sees them too.

If he does, maybe he can understand that I am just a man. Is it possible that he is just a man? Maybe he can understand that war is pointless and it must stop.

Jewish, all this has another dimension." His personal connection to the concept of the story, revealed through inclusion of his own family photographs, is metaphorical – we too can empathise with the character; the photographs represent the families of each reader. As Serge says, "the book is for everybody – whoever you are it's always the same story."

The power of this award-winning book, promoted by Amnesty International and exhibited in the United Nations headquarters in New York, lies largely in the synthesis of images and text. "I try to respect the text," Serge reveals. "I follow the words. I can't do another story at the same time for this book." The narrative is a vehicle for many issues – hate, propaganda and the nature of the enemy – revealing the power of the individual to make change. Simultaneously, it asserts the power of illustration to impact upon the ubiquitous challenges of our times. As Serge points out, "I wasn't thinking this is a book for kids, it's a book for all people."

Serge Bloch was born and lives in France.

I have made a mistake. There are lions at night, and they can see in the dark. I just spotted one and must stay still.

I am lucky. The lion is leaving.

The enemy is over there but I have never seen him. Every morning, I shoot at him. Then he shoots at me.

We both stay hidden the rest of the day, waiting.

The Enemy
Spreads written by Davide Cali and illustrated by Serge Bloch, published by Schwartz & Wade, 2009

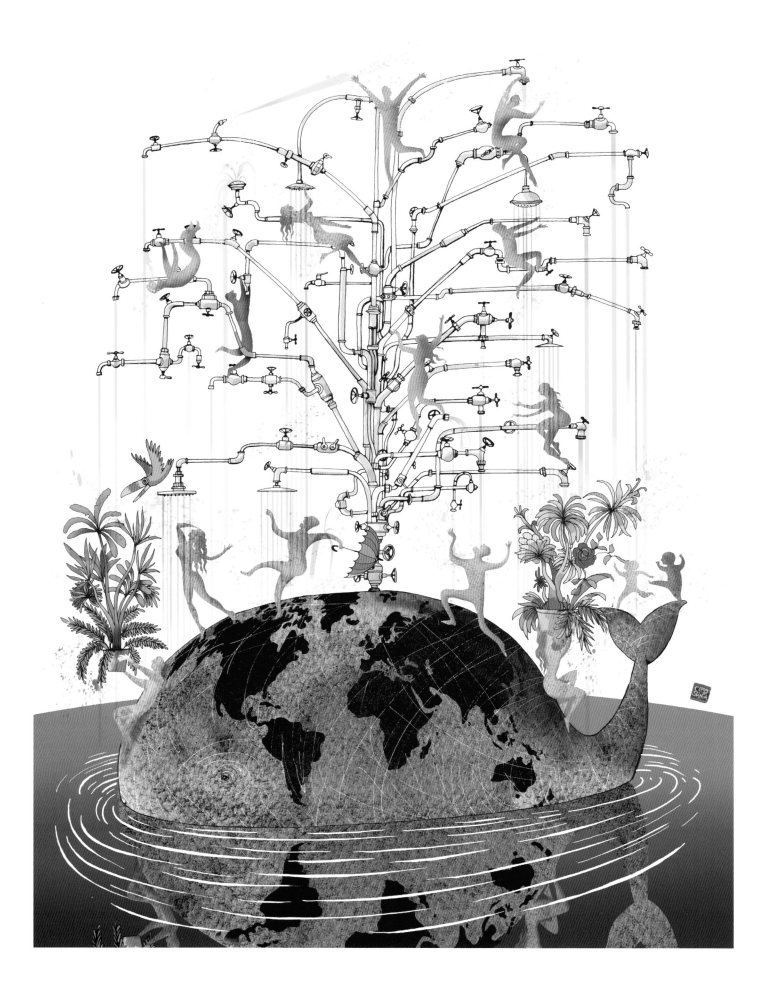

Carlo Stanga
Water – UNESCO poster

Although not immediately overt, the skills and attitude that underpin the descriptive and expressive images for which Carlo Stanga is generally recognised, with their strong architectural bias, are latently inherent in *Water*, commissioned by UNESCO (United Nations Educational, Scientific and Cultural Organization) as a poster for its annual conference in 2011. Carlo says of the piece, "I also create illustrations without architecture, even though the architectural rhythm is always present somehow in my work." This image demonstrates how a visual language can extend to fulfil unexpected functions across eclectic contexts. The brief provided an opportunity for Carlo to create conceptual imagery marrying his strong aesthetic with symbolic and metaphorical content dealing with an issue of global significance. "I love beauty and I think the artworks should transmit a pleasant sensation, but at the same time I aim to combine this with a strong message. I am still looking for a good balance."

The poster aims to encourage sustainability, thoughtful consumption and intelligent and democratic distribution of water. It celebrates its preciousness as a commodity and as an essential and life-sustaining element. The image is constructed from interconnected components each with a specific narrative function in the communication of these points. Of his approach to the message Carlo says, "I have to find the keys to express the idea in a deep and sympathetic way."

His choice of visual metaphors results in a divided but conjoined image in which the base can be viewed as what Carlos refers to as, "the archetypal part: the ancient and natural aspect of water as an element deeply connected with life". The whale is representational, depicted as the biggest animal on earth, living in the water, and holding a deeper connotation: "a mammal that symbolises the deepest idea of the mystery of life, as a sacred icon, a totem. The whale is the water itself, the ancient goddess that, just like a mother, gave life to us and constantly does so again and again. It is something we cannot do without." The reflection metamorphoses to form the earth, made whole through water, a perfect natural form independent of, and preceding, mankind.

In contrast the top section of the image relates to what Carlos refers to as, "the artificial part, distributing and conveying the water jet coming naturally from the whale." This system of pipes represents mankind's intervention with water and the responsibility of organising its consumption.

Water
Poster design, UNESCO (Unesco Italian Commission), 2011

"Most of the time my work is characterised by accurate details in complex and whimsical urban views. Over the years I have begun to tire of a purely representational approach and I need to express a stronger concept within my images."

Given Carlo's background his approach is unsurprising. The image is built on a strong framework of design, the composition endorsing the notion inherent within the theme of the essential balance between man and nature. This aesthetic draws on what Carlo refers to as, "a natural inclination to construct". He clarifies that "in this illustration the tree pipes have a structure, with a rhythm and a hierarchy. If you like, you can also figure that this is an X-ray of a plumbing system. So the architecture is present in this illustration, but it is transparent."

Colour is used deliberately in the UNESCO *Water* image to exaggerate the sense of opposites working in harmony. The line quality, similar to that found in architectural and engineering drawings before the prevalence of digital media, is what Carlos describes as "the first component of my language." The colour and softer watercolour bring a more lyrical quality to the idea. "The symbolic meaning for me is definitely psychological. Colours mean feelings, compared to black and white that has a rational, technical and cerebral sense. This combines with colour that signifies life."

There is a balance also between the aesthetic and conceptual nature of the image and an additional poetic substance which Carlo says emerges from the theme. "It was spontaneous to be both conceptual and emotional. The theme itself is strong and deep and beautiful." These qualities, added to the optimism of the illustration, contribute to its appeal. "In this case it would have been easy to recall tragic situations where people are suffering on the earth, because of lack of water, but I decided to stay in happy and serene lines."

It is usual for Carlo to be mindful of the graphic context in which his imagery will exist, and his decisions are influenced by the colour, shape and relative position of type. As he says, "an illustration has to have a dialogue with the context, its final destination, and has to work with it. This isn't high art, it's located art."

Although its primary function was as a poster, and later a magazine cover, the ideas explored in the image have universal and ongoing relevance, beyond the original commissioned context. Its statement transcends cultural boundaries. It is art positioned firmly in the wider context of vital and ongoing world issues.

Carlo Stanga lives in Italy and Berlin.

Underground Gallery
(An example of other commissioned work, for which Carlo is also recognised, without specific issues-based content.)
Poster design: MTA, New York, 2010.
Art Director: Lydia Bradshaw

A Monster Calls
Written by Patrick Ness from an idea by Siobhan Dowd,
images by Jim Kay, published by Walker Books, 2011

"What is frightening is what you don't see
– what you don't see is usually hidden in
shadow. As soon as you reveal it, you
lose that power."

Jim Kay
A Monster Calls

"When I was working on the first major scene I immediately imagined a triangle leaning against a square – it's about the collision and tension between an ancient primeval force and a contemporary issue," says Jim Kay, referring to the menacing image of the dark looming figure now synonymous with *A Monster Calls*. The illustration is one from the series for the award-winning and heart-rending story by Patrick Ness, in which the teenager Conor is tormented by visits from a monster – a hybrid figure metamorphosed from the yew tree from outside his window. The story blurs the boundary between his nightmare and the tormenting reality of the impending and certain death of Conor's mother.

Jim's beguiling images are now recognised as a distinct force weaving inseparably through the visceral text, but he recalls his initial hesitancy when approached to consider the commission. "I didn't think the story should be illustrated as it is written with such clarity and is such a personal book." This is a reminder of the complex relationships operating between narrative and image. As well as the function that images perform when connected to text there is a potential for these two languages to jar. As Jim puts it, "I didn't know if illustration would detract from the story – there was a risk of the illustrations breaking the rhythm of the writing."

His intuitive intention was to follow an instinct to provide visual props and describe urban spaces in images that reflected the text – what he describes as "scene setting – creating the stage for the actual story". It was the astute art direction provided by Ben Norland at Walker Books, who Jim describes as a "mediator" between himself and the author, which led to the more direct illustration he did of the book's main scenes. "He told me to embrace the story and go off on tangents."

Jim exploits the narrative connotations held within inanimate objects. "I love forensic photos of crime scenes from the 1930s, the shadow of something that's happened, the idea of events that have passed." This results in images he describes as "suggestive rather than descriptive", containing objects such as upturned chairs and empty urban spaces, "human, but devoid of human presence".

He acknowledges the part played by the audience in the full definition of the meaning of the pictures. "I tend not to describe my characters in detail, so readers can identify and slip into the space," he says. The monster, the pivotal character in this story, has distinct functions. As a metaphor created by the author it signifies the maelstrom of Conor's bewildering and overwhelming emotions. Gravitating between being human and tree, its shifting visual state is also what Jim describes as "a barometer for the mood of the story". It is a form both beguiling and terrifying – its compelling nature born from 'green man' mythologies. Whilst Jim acknowledges a long-term personal fascination with this archetype, his reflection of it is neither conscious nor deliberate. The connection with the audience is expressive rather than conceptual or rational. He explains, "I become so blinkered when I'm working, I don't think of the allegory of it, what others take from it, or what I would pass on. It's for myself."

Engaging the viewer as collaborator in the visual process, however, is revealed clearly in Jim's initial concept during the evolution of the Monster character. Borrowed from Rorschach inkblots, a method of psychological evaluation used by psychologists to

examine the personality characteristics and emotional functioning of their patients, Jim's intention in the developmental work was for the reader to search for meaning in ink patterns, each bringing an individual interpretation to the image, one shaped by their particular psychology. Working in harmony with the text this visual process plays cleverly on the ambiguity of whether the monster is real or imagined.

The sensitive handling of tone and polemic contrast that contributes to the arresting power of the images, a production challenge for the publisher, emanates in part from Jim's immersion in the world of old movies. The images make reference to films such as F.W. Murnau's 1922 film *Nosferatu*. The dark areas provide an ambiguity that forces the viewer to engage with the pieces. "What is frightening is what you don't see – what you don't see is usually hidden in shadow. As soon as you reveal it you lose that power." As well as the atmosphere having importance, the debt to film comes through the book's sense of pacing, sequence and the cinematic interpretation of the narrative, "I'm interested in the progression of time in the book – the reading of left to right to get a sense of progression through the pages of text."

There is an autobiographical aspect to the work, which subconsciously reflects the particular bleak conditions the illustrator worked in at the time. Significantly, nature was a force – "I couldn't draw in detail because my fingers were too cold!" – as well as permeating his aesthetic. "Everything was in black and white," Jim explains. "The trees and buildings were black, and when the snow came it bleached out mid-tones – like shooting with a low-quality camera."

With layers of print, charcoal drawing, mark-making and ink textures, all composited digitally, the images exude a tactility and an expressionistic rawness empathetically dealing with issues of fear, loss and the healing of emotional pain. Surprisingly, because he imagined creating a set of prints for the book Jim feels the work is incomplete. What is certain is the power of this book, and that the continuing accolades the extraordinary illustrations receive from the reading public, and from the worlds of publishing, art, design and medicine, are clearly deserved.

Jim Kay lives in Scotland.

Spread and image from
A Monster Calls

04 Off The Printed Page

Illustration moves in many directions, not only embracing the ever-expanding opportunities provided by new media, but also transcending barriers which once separated practices within art and design. Increasingly moving off the printed page, it takes in site-based imagery in the form of installations for retail and shows, murals and exhibition design, and artwork placed on existing structures, reaching audiences in direct and unexpected ways; work created for the digital environment of websites, gaming, commercial and artistic interactive projects, film and music video; and illustration on the multidimensional facets of the fashion world, from textiles to the catwalk show.

Three-dimensional illustration can stretch from carved creatures such as Emma Houlston's monsters, part of a comprehensive illustrative campaign for fashion brand Mulberry, to limited-edition collectable vinyl figures like Nathan Jurevicius's Dievas Dunny, bringing the symbolism of folklore into a contemporary genre.

Fashion, always on the lookout for something new, frequently employs the work of illustrators, who can bring a fresh outlook and add appeal to clothing and make individual statements. Fashion pioneer Barbara Hulanicki, who formed fashion house Biba in the 1960s, still returns to illustration, applying her distinctive character drawings to a range of T-shirt designs.

The opportunities for illustration to engage and communicate within digital platforms stretch ahead in an unending stream. With a growing amount of downloadable and web-based content, digital creativity is a premium element for companies and brands wishing to catch the attention of potential customers. With the 'worlds' created for Adobe's Creative Suite, Alex Jenkins and his team worked closely with the client to produce an interactive website full of imagery which engages through imagined environments and characters while delivering pertinent information about the product.

With the increasing prevalence of illustration incorporated into a physical environment, Kristjana S. Williams's collaged prints, presented to the visiting public of an art and design museum to interact with and adapt via an app, involve technology in the visitor experience. Whilst offering a creative experience celebrating the versatility of illustration, the project also raises issues surrounding plagiarism of artwork.

Animation has developed with increasing sophistication, certainly in feature films. It works effectively using various visual languages when employed across music video, promotional films and advertising. Bands looking for strong visual accompaniment to a song draw on artists to provide a unique element to take their music to a wider audience. Lesley Barnes brings narrative, pattern and charm to her video for Belle and Sebastian's *I Didn't See it Coming*, constructing characters and scenarios which complement the song as well as inhabiting their own world. Illustrators such as Lesley increasingly bring additional skills to their visual and intellectual approach, incorporating design, animation and typographic elements to expand their language of commercial art.

Whether used within advertising campaigns or as part of urban regeneration, site-based art can transform a space and has the potential to enrich an environment, whether urban or not, communicating to and engaging with an audience. Lucy McLauchlan's mural applied to an historical building far from an urban environment reflects poignantly on the history and stories of its remote location, while the exhibition pieces created by Jill Calder memorably entertain and educate museum visitors with their playful depictions of flora and fauna.

Transcending the historical positioning of illustration, contemporary practice now bends around buildings, moves across apps and animations, encouraging viewers to be more than passive observers, interacting and contributing explicitly, and all with intelligence and style.

Obrestad Lighthouse mural
Commissioned by Hå Gamle Prestegard Arts and Culture Centre.
Located in Jæren, Norway, 2011. Main photo supplied by Ingunn Nord-Varhaug, Curator.

Lucy McLauchlan
Obrestad Lighthouse

Site-based artworks painted onto buildings, usually those occupying public spaces, have gained cultural acceptance as a respected art form often referred to as urban art. This mural, commissioned for the Obrestad Lighthouse situated on a dramatic piece of Norwegian coastline, confounds any preconceptions of what this broad and evolving genre entails. It represents a marriage of cultures: steeped in Nordic history the lighthouse, built in 1873, is radically transformed by imagery more commonly associated with a distinctive urban culture.

For artist Lucy McLauchlan this piece epitomises the work for which she is celebrated. Recognised and respected globally for the bold monochromatic graphic patterns, interwoven with emblems that are used to 'wrap' buildings and walls, her images transform structures and surfaces in many locations around the world. Although the idiom of street art and certain dimensions of its aesthetic have been adopted by mainstream advertising to reach particular consumer groups, this piece, in common with most urban art, is democratic, uninhibited by commercial constraints and thus able to be encountered freely.

Although the absence of a particular commercial function or target audience provided Lucy with a certain creative freedom, the logistics of scale and the ergonomics of the space, as well as the extreme climate and surroundings, constrained the selection and development of visual content dictating and encompassing what she painted. She describes this as "allowing the building and its environment to be part of the image and its message", a reminder that unlike most areas of illustration the physicality in the process of making site-based work is a major factor in the visual outcome." She recalls, "I spent a week in the hands of

the weather waiting for a glimpse where the cold wet winds and fog off the North Sea parted long enough to get up in the cherry picker. I couldn't help but feel the strength of the elements surrounding and covering me."

Although urban art often infers a political or social intention, with a building acting as a platform for a particular message, Lucy's process was a reactive one and the work "improvised", with the location dictating the meaning and significance. Despite being a national landmark protected by Norway's Cultural Heritage Act, the commissioners allowed Lucy to create without any restrictions on content. The subsequent meaning inherent in the imagery is subtle. Although she works with little or no pre-planning, narratives form as part of the journey as she paints. This is what she describes as "absorbing what's happening around me and translating it, whether consciously or subconsciously".

Although Lucy says the imagery has no direct meanings, in deploying the fluid and repeated motifs of birds, leaves and figures that have evolved from what she describes as "partially simple aesthetic qualities mixed with more symbolic thought and messages of life around me", Obrestad Lighthouse provided an opportunity to include the iconic organic forms that symbolise nature – what she refers to as "one of the few constants in our world". As Lucy says, "I was simply reflecting the power and beauty of the earth's natural elements that I felt push around me."

Within this work Lucy also reflected on the rich history of the site and specifically the occupation of the lighthouse by German soldiers during World War II. "Paintings of exotic girls in faraway lands still exist on the basement's walls. A primal dream hidden away." The war bunkers remaining on the site and old Viking burial mounds in the near vicinity, along with the

dramatic coastal setting, were both evocative and stimulating. "Life, death, Norsemen, Nazis, the film Valhalla Rising: all were in mind when painting there. It seeped through into the imagery, leaving a narrative that wraps around the whole structure, continually."

This commission was notably created to be seen away from a commercially print-based or gallery environment – art encountered in its original form. The format extends beyond three dimensions. The building itself offers a permanent and unchanging surface and form, which influenced the design and placement of the imagery but also the space it occupies, while the transient forces of nature impact upon the way it is perceived. Enjoying the piece is essentially a sensory experience. As Lucy reminds us, it is intended to be interacted with as one element in a broader vista: "the wind blows the viewer around to witness the painting simultaneously with the sounds, smell and strength of the North Sea nudging you along".

Wherever the impetus comes from, the motivation for site-based art is often a process of physical transformation of the site. Referring to her own practice Lucy says, "often a space will catch your eye, it's obvious, needing something or someone to change its surface. Having said that, I think there's something within human nature, an urge to leave a mark, whether it's in public or private places. Secrets to be discovered."

Lucy McLauchlan was born and lives in the UK.

Todo es posible
Birmingham City Library, UK, 2011.
Photo supplied by the artist.

Lucy is commissioned and invited to participate in projects internationally.
Dead space is a project conceived and produced by EC-Arts www.ec-arts.com. The project
is an experimental series of public art exhibitions to create accessible art within the public
realm, supported and sponsored by The Royal Society For Arts West Midlands, Central Library,
Birmingham City Council and Birmingham City University

Lucy painting Obrestad Lighthouse,
Hå Gamle Prestegard and Nuart, 2011.
Photograph: Elizabeth Croft

Garden Detectives exhibition
Design by Stuart Kerr, Exhibition Design and National
Museums of Scotland in-house design team,
The National Museum of Scotland, 2009

"It was like theatre design."

Jill Calder
Garden Detectives exhibition

Designed to be encountered and experienced within a large museum space in which touch and smell contributed to the physical experience and understanding of the images, this dynamic set of works undertaken by illustrator Jill Calder for the Garden Detectives Exhibition at The National Museum of Scotland in Edinburgh, tangibly reveals the power of illustration to exist, "off the printed page". Her drawings and illustration of all sorts of flora and fauna – insects, flowers, bees and mammals – are at the heart of the exhibition. Content and form combine to create a fascinating and enchanting outside world designed to entertain and educate a young participating audience in ways that went beyond looking and reading.

Being asked to produce illustration as part of this exhibition to celebrate Darwin's 200th anniversary was initially "terrifying" for Jill, not because the subject or the context were beyond her proven scope but because the commission required accurate drawing of the subject when her work is characteristically expressive. "I love drawing and I love freedom so it was a fantastic experience, but I did have to check they knew I'm not a botanical illustrator." In her interpretations of the subjects the museum was looking for a synthesis of both objective and subjective content. "They gave me some reference and I found some myself. I also drew from life when I could." Whilst being biologically accurate the illustrations still carry all the hallmarks of Jill's individual visual language, with vibrant colour and fluid lines.

The illustrator's personal input is a vital ingredient in the interpretation of a subject, and Jill infuses these examples with life. "The narrative is very important to me. I need a story, whether written or not." The stories in this work are a subtle expression of her personality and humour. They remind us also that the meaning of an image can come from outside the frame, its references to people, places and ideas unseen. At first glance it's a pretty picture, says Jill (referring to the mural on the previous page) but the stone wall with the trug left behind becomes the story of someone who has gone to get a cup of tea. And the mouse comes to see what's happening. "I make it into something that could have happened naturally. It doesn't matter if anyone notices or not – it entertains me." The narrative result conveys a sense of the exhibition as, in part, a larger-than-life interactive picture book.

The work relies on a shared sense of the expressive meaning of colour. "It was important. I was seeing it as summer, it was very much about being cheerful. I was thinking about colour and light." Like the installations, the images were also constructed, structured, according to Jill's informed sense of how pictorial forms interconnect and interact with the audience. "I make quite subconscious decisions about colour but the balance of the image has to be right."

The project is significant because it both dispels the myth of museums as sacred places and shows natural history illustration needn't be an arid or static art form. The exhibition was more than hands-on, incorporating spaces to be climbed through, and images to be assembled, deconstructed and sniffed. The boundaries between the exhibits and her artwork were sometimes ignored. Jill recalls, "Some of the taxidermy from the museum was included in interesting ways: a quirky shed had a fox on the roof peeking down – it was like theatre design."

These images reveal how technically specific information, such as this about the animals and their habitats, can be translated into new forms. Jill describes the objectives of the work as "educational", and this exciting and multilayered environment encourages children to "go outside and explore, be curious". Play is central to learning and discovery and illustration is instrumental to this activity, contributing vitally to the project's overwhelming success.

Working within a large space, addressing specific and evolving objectives about how her images would be used, required close and ongoing liaison with a skilled team that included curators, exhibition designers and graphic designers. Although Jill made the drawings back in her studio the project is a reminder that making illustration is a collaborative endeavour. The technical properties of the application, the logistics of space and scale and audience participation, are parts of the creative equation that have to be considered alongside the aesthetics of the work.

As well as collaboration in the making, like a piece of theatre the work comes to life and gains fuller meaning because of human intervention. It has been recognised for an award by the Association of Illustrators, but the full value of the work can only be measured in the reactions of the many children visiting the museum and its ongoing impact on their understanding and appreciation of the natural world.

Jill Calder lives in Scotland, UK.

Images from the **Garden Detectives exhibition**
The National Museum of Scotland, 2009.
Above: 3D Hedgerow, 2.5m long x 1.5 high x 1m wide

Monster characters and padlock balloons
(below, opposite) used on the catwalk and in
promotions for their Autumn/Winter Collection,
Mulberry, 2012

Emma Houlston
Mulberry Monster campaign

The fashion brand Mulberry is associated with upmarket design classics – luxury British fashion that is coveted the world over. The brand conjures up images of elegant models clad in exquisite attire and fine fabrics, but it is a world in which Big Monster was also brought into existence by his creator, illustrator Emma Houlston. Illustration and fashion fuse in this commission to provoke narratives and fantasies, a glimpse into enchanting worlds. Emma describes the brief. "They asked me to design a range of characters and I created a 'family' of monsters, each with a different personality that would be used as part of their campaign for their collection for autumn/winter 2012."

The illustrations have been applied in many ways: on fabric for the collection and monumentally transformed into large three-dimensional characters sculpted out of polystyrene by a model-making company. The creatures stand proud on the fashion catwalk, a central feature of the highly staged and imaginatively choreographed fashion experience. Closely resembling a theatre production, this event, like most high-fashion shows, combined lighting and sound to create an ambience which brought the monster world to life for a select audience of fashionistas. Emma describes the opportunity to create the character designs for these giant 3D forms as being, "scary. It was a challenge because I had to work so quickly. It was fun."

"It was a trail of inspiration with the fashion designers at one end and illustration at the other. We met in the middle."

These benign, oversized creatures are awe-inspiring and evoke curiosity. They are not clothed but they are a reminder that fashion is often rooted in fantasy and escapism. The characters borrow from various mythologies, as Emma explains: "I think the monsters are like giant magpies collecting beautiful things and taking them to their nest. They are friendly and not scary at all." The landscape the creatures inhabit is adorned with oversized, inflated golden padlocks, designed by Emma with reference to the Mulberry padlock that is an accessory featured on some of their products. "It's a bit like the Midas touch where everything turns to gold. The monsters lead you into another world where anything can happen."

Although they are not connected to any specific story or narrative, there are obvious references to *Where the Wild Things Are*, by Maurice Sendak, and *Not Now, Bernard,* by David McKee. There's a sense of enchantment and adventure and a reminder of childhood, where illustration can be a door to fabled lands, a magic that through these creatures becomes associated with the Mulberry brand.

The technical constraints of the fashion show and the challenge for the monster models to work spatially meant that there were very specific requirements to be factored into the character development from the beginning. "The characters had to be practical for the catwalk: the monsters had to work from the back as well as the front – they couldn't just be lumps of fur as the audience around the back also needed to get the feel of them. I went through the process of trying variations, adding tails, different eyes and teeth. I knew it was going to be vectored up but didn't know how the detail would work." Looking at the intricately drawn, stylised fur on each beast it's easy to believe that the initial connection between monsters and fashion was based almost entirely on their common textures. "The autumn/winter collection features particular materials, such as the coats made from Mongolian fur. The monster idea came from that, and I looked closely at animals like goats' and yaks' fur for the drawings."

"This is a spiraling world of work," Emma says, marvelling at the inventiveness with which they have been subsequently used in other formats as part of an ongoing campaign, in which the images have been applied to bags, cushions, T-shirts, towels – even a lilo floating on a swimming pool for the Mulberry Coachella pool party. As pieces of surface pattern and textile design the images have found new functions and new audiences that perceive, use and interact with them in new ways. These products have been a source of delight for Emma. "Usually my world as an illustrator doesn't pass through the world of fashion, but with the Mulberry monster the end of the illustration was just the beginning."

Emma Houlston lives and works in London, UK.

Monster characters and padlock balloons
(above and opposite) used on the catwalk and in promotions for their Autumn/Winter Collection, Mulberry, 2012

Dievas packaging art
for Kidrobot, 2011

Nathan Jurevicius
Dievas Dunny figure

ievas, created by Nathan Jurevicius, epitomises the phenomenon of limited-edition designer toys that was born in Japan in the 1990s, and which are now seen internationally as collectable art products, in this case distributed by market leaders Kidrobot. Nathan's customisation and transformation of a standard 8-inch (20cm) Dunny, a rabbit-like form covered with black flock, metamorphoses into a highly desirable object.

Throughout history objects have been invested with value and meaning, and with its moon-like eyes *Dievas* pays homage to the owl, a protagonist in numerous global mythologies. "The owl is a great-looking creature – it's in the eyes. It's iconic as a bird, and has a back story." In common with many of Nathan's characters the piece draws upon his early childhood, in which folklore and spirituality had an impact. "My grandfather was a great influence. He gave me books with fairytales from Eastern Europe. Religious texts also give me a basis to develop my own mythology."

Although it is what Nathan describes as "a mash of Australian, Lithuanian and Eastern folklore", this particular character reflects the ambiguity of metaphorical meaning that comes from cross-cultural interpretation. Traditionally perceived as a symbol for wisdom, knowledge and wealth in ancient Egyptian, Celtic and Hindu cultures, the owl is also recognised as a guardian of the underworld. The Dievas, or deity according to Lithuanian legend, adopts its form to escort souls on their final spiritual journey. It is seen

Dievas Dunny for Kidrobot
Limited-edition collectable vinyl toy, 2011

Misko
Wooden mini figure series,
Kidrobot, 2012

as ruler of the night and associated with sinister forces of spirit worlds, and this contributes to the potent mysticism of this piece. "I really like the dual personality – that the metaphor is both for bad and for good." Understanding these narratives isn't vital to appreciation of this figure. Nathan elaborates: "What's great is that the object can stand on its own." Referring to the packaging, which with its ornate geometric decoration is instantly recognisable as a piece of his work, he adds, "the context gives insight and makes the viewer appreciate and understand on a greater level. Others may take it on board just as it is."

The notion of ambiguity and Janus-like qualities – challenging archetypes and provoking reaction beyond initial face value – are threads running through Nathan's work. This is evident most famously within the imaginative, highly successful life of his most acclaimed character, Scarygirl (seen overleaf). She inhabits a dreamlike world populated with a cast of complex

and surprising characters. "Beautiful things can be dangerous," says Nathan of the edginess in some of his work. "What seems scary can just be a preconceived idea of something fearful – in reality it may be the kindest, least harmful creature."

Work across different platforms and in 3D is often underpinned by 2D imagery and for Nathan this is pivotal to his versatility, who reveals, "I look at drawing as the first stepping stone." In the case of the Dievas a similar character existed as part of a one-off two-dimensional art print that was originally inspired from a new story based on an exhibition and toy series called Peleda. The Peleda world is now in production as an online game and TV series for the Australian Broadcasting Corporation. Strong pattern, vibrant colour and a sense of magic realism creates a strong visual identity whatever final form the work takes. "Achieving that usually requires collaboration," he says of this versatility, explaining, "I come up with

Opposite:
Mountain Queen
Cover for *90+10* magazine, 2012

the stories and concept." Handing over aspects of the technical process and production to other creative people, working in teams with them, is something that Nathan values. "I like to commission and work with people who are better than I am, people who appreciate and understand." In the case of the Dievas the client's involvement was limited to the selection of the character and final manufacture of the sculpture.

The practice of illustration increasingly involves crossing platforms – Nathan is a good example of this: creating drawings, animations, toys, games, installations and books. "I like my work to keep changing, like my life," he says. "I go off on multiple tangents – I accept it will get bigger. I like the idea of worlds expanding. I don't want to keep it small." As an example, since its creation in 2001, Scarygirl has evolved from being a collectable toy into an international brand. Her stories are also told through limited-edition vinyl toys, designer products, interactive games and a graphic novel. Nathan is also in active development for a feature film with Passion Pictures Australia.

The connection between personal and commercial work is important. Although Nathan works for a range of clients and enjoys substantial mainstream success, the authorial dimension of his practice is vital. His capacity as a storyteller is nourished by international travel and enjoyment of cultural diversity and a desire to explore ideas. "I feel like I still have one foot in indie circles – I start independently and then go commercial." Having vision and a sense of enquiry can lead to unforeseen discoveries and Nathan optimises these. "I enjoy the freedom. I sometimes make a one-off piece and what starts as a sideline becomes a world. Unfortunately, I then want to create an environment and then a universe."

Nathan Jurevicius was born in Australia and lives in Canada.

"One thing sparks another and
then builds into something large.
Sometimes the small things surprise."

Scarygirl
Limitied-edition resin figure produced with
Bigshot Toyworks, 2010

City Vision
From **The Adventures of Scarygirl** by
Nathan Jurevicicius, published by Allen &
Unwin, 2012

Barbara Hulanicki
Tickled Pink T-Shirts

The T-shirt has become the art gallery of the street and is a form of communication and expression for both artist and wearer. "The illustration drawing I do is tremendously felt," explains Barbara Hulanicki. Consequently, the fashion-based images emanating from this dynamic woman, who is drawn to "pretty girls with lovely faces and skinny elongated bodies", have a real life and soul.

These drawings are illustrations for a series of limited-edition T-shirts for the fashion range George at ASDA – a British supermarket chain. Commissioned for their Tickled Pink campaign which raises awareness for the Breast Cancer organisation, they represent a particular visual idiom which has typified much of Barbara's fashion career, helping it to enjoy renewed and increased popularity through mass availability. The characters are resonant of those iconic, doe-eyed models, and have a pervasive sense of the opulence which epitomised Biba, the fashion business she set up with her late husband in the 1960s. This was a time of rebelliousness and daring, conveyed through a brand with which her name has an enduring association. It's clear that Biba is not something that she looks back to; instead it is, as she says, "part of something always inside of me". Fashion is cyclical, and the intuitive aesthetic approach has resonance today for both the illustrator and those who are drawn to wear the T-shirt, even if the spirit of rebellion is long past. "Fashion moves so fast and some things disappear, some things

Girl with Roses
Design for T-shirt for the ASDA Tickled Pink campaign, commissioned by George for ASDA, 2009

Limited edition T-shirts by George at ASDA for their
Tickled Pink breast cancer awareness campaign

"I like to break boredom – to find a little place where the boredom stops where you can insert ideas into."

stay. It usually takes on the mood of what's going on," she explains.

Barbara draws from an inner core. She isn't conscious of creating archetypes, but her drawings reflect her mood, and subconsciously with their beauty, elegance and strength are parts of herself. Her characters embody a myriad of influences: she describes how as a child she watched her mother "putting herself together", and also being immersed in old movies of the 1940s with their beautiful leading ladies. They reflect the Art Nouveau images she researched for commissions very early in her career, and the Pre-Raphaelite women populating the paintings of Burne-Jones and Rossetti which were part of her childhood. It is the qualities reflected by these figures that are archetypal, contributing to the enduring appeal of her contemporary drawings and their relevance for a campaign such as this where the positive depiction of femininity in women dealing with breast cancer is latent.

When drawing, Barbara captures a moment which embodies her feelings at that time. Her fluid drawing seems spontaneous – she refers to herself as a conduit to a dynamic force she describes as, "a big cycle, a wheel which I automatically and psychically follow, knowing I have to find the one right moment". Images such as the illustrations here are the result of a process of fastidious editing and selection, and a search for a certain minimalism that comes from a lifetime of "looking, and storing everything in my head".

This illustration is quite different from the sketchy pencil drawings which Barbara uses to "unlock ideas" as part of her design process for architectural and interior design. She explains, "I hop around so much on different projects, so they require different ways of putting things down onto the paper." Unlike the design work, which she says, "is largely done in the head and verbally", with a particular function of communicating ideas, the fashion illustrations have their own existence: each illustration stands as a canvas autonomous

of other narratives, words or expectations, and consequently, as Barbara says, "I have real freedom".

Much of Barbara Huklanicki's work across fashion, architecture, interior design and illustration is a manifestation of beauty, and although the T-shirt has increasingly become a vehicle for overt personal statements, here it subtly sums up fashion with its connotations and narratives of style and escapism. She is fascinated by what she describes as "other people's vision", when they will interpret what she has created in a unique way. In that vein each person who sees her illustration plays their own part in defining and contributing to its meaning and appreciation.

Barbara Huklanicki, a founder of Biba, was born in Poland, has lived in the UK and now lives in the USA.

This page and opposite
Tee shirt designs for '**Art of the Tee**'
line for fashion brand bebe, 2009.
Bebe natural canvas bag, 2009

Kristjana S. Williams
Victoria & Albert Museum
interactive print journey

This photograph documents a design experiment instigated by the British Galleries at the Victoria & Albert Museum as part of the London Design Festival in 2011. The exhibition focused around a series of four interactive prints created by Kristjana S. Williams. The artist created an immersive, theatrical environment, part installation, part applied illustration, in which members of the public could explore the nature of construction and application of decorative images using elements pulled from her own artwork.

For the commission her existing designs were specifically adapted and applied to wallpaper, fabric, clothing and furniture designed by George Smith – her imagery was all-pervasive in this purposefully designed 3D space. The museum visitors were invited to use an iPad to create alternative designs and visualise their application in various contexts, a process that entailed lifting fragments, modifying them and bringing a new identity to her motifs. This is a practice which closely mirrors Kristjana's own methodology and mimics her image construction. "My own work is based on borrowed images and collage," she confirms. The ethos of the project was fuelled by personal interests which include "applying, wrapping, technology, motion, holograms, and experiential art – creating a whole world to inhabit".

This commission is a reminder of the ubiquitous and multidimensional functionality of illustration. Here it is revealed to be a flexible type of surface pattern. Articulated on textiles the pattern influences the perception of forms, such as the figure and furniture, while as wallpaper it creates ambience and suggests narrative.

It is content that gives value to these surfaces. What underpins and makes Kristjana's work distinctive is her intuitive imagination fuelling the mysterious aesthetic of her imagery. The Gothic worlds she creates rely on digital manipulation to amalgamate the fragments of Victorian engravings, natural-history prints and her own photography. She renders these with intense enhanced colour, engineering a sense of exotic hyperrealism. Inspired by the myths and stories told to her by her family during childhood in her native Iceland, she now connects her imaginative output to these early years. "Growing up in what I then thought was a bleak landscape gives my work a darker edge."

She relishes these lush environments populated by hybrid beasts, trees, jewel-like flowers and butterflies, recognising that "they aren't dreamlike – they are what I see. They are convincing, they could be real, but of course they aren't. Mine is a fantasy world." The success of this work is due in part also to the primal impact made by the flora and fauna which have become her trademarks, and the symmetrical organisation of elements reflecting a natural structural order such as that of the skeletons of the leaves which she has studied. "Trees, flowers, butterflies, animals and plants all share the same lines and fuse together. Nature gifts them to me to work with." There are no people inhabiting this fantasy world because, "they aren't interesting to me, they don't sit with the natural elements". Both their absence and the juxtaposition of Victorian and contemporary elements gives her pieces a timeless quality; disconnecting images from a specific place or culture is a factor in their potential longevity and versatility.

This commission was a harbinger of the evolution that in recent years has occurred within the broad area of decorative illustration that Kristjana's career is part of: moving from a predominantly fashion-related platform where images were designed specifically

An 'Interactive Print Journey' (Lear Gaukur Journey), the London Design Festival, Victoria and Albert Museum, 2011. Photograph supplied by the artist

to be applied to clothing, wallpapers, textiles and surfaces, to an environment where these now exist as pieces independent of other forms, in which "they have become stories and pieces with a meaning of their own."

The latent connotations inherent in the project have deeper resonance for artists and designers operating in a digital age. Readily available, sophisticated software packages permit both image appropriation and invention as well as facilitating their distribution globally. Kristjana reflects on this, "People have said I was mad to allow the public to play with my images but I was lifting the mystery about how an image can be made. I'm always pushing forward and play is important to me, too."

The project raises topical issues about plagiarism, copyright and visual literacy as well as design prowess and ownership, subjects with broad cultural currency. From these emerge latent questions to consider: What right does any of us have to take another's image and transform its form and function? What is the value of collaboration? When does an image cease being an illustration?

Kristjana S. Williams was born in Iceland and lives in London, UK.

Fjoluraut PALL
Limited edition archival giclée print, 2012

Fuglar og fidrildin PALL
Limited edition archival giclée print, 2012

Rosar Hjartar Tre
Limited edition archival giclée print, 2012

"For me this was a great job, because it was
a cross between animation and illustration."

Alex Jenkins
Adobe Creative Suite interactive website

The online environment is a fertile ground for brands wishing to communicate with their desired audience, and although innovation is important when reaching out visually, retaining a core of storytelling alongside the eye-catching elements can produce a more effective result. When Adobe launched their Creative Suite 2.3 software package, their US agency, Goodby, Silverstein & Partners, proposed an interactive promotional website, combining the work of two artists onto each of three imagined worlds which would individually embody the new tools available within the upgraded Suite.

Unit 9 in London were charged with creating the site, and animator and Creative Director, Alex Jenkins, took the agency's idea and enhanced the concept and functions of the new site with narrative elements. The result was a charming, intriguing, humorous and informative piece. The idea that this promotional site should directly convey a substantial amount of information was challenged, as this could already be accessed from the official Creative Suite site.

Three themed worlds were created for the site to represent different aspects of the functionality of Creative Suite software: *I love my Gut* – about gut instinct; *Must.Work.Fast* – about intuition and efficiency; and *Impossible? Possible* – about malleability, flexible workflows and collaboration. The agency's broad concept was to present two selected artists and create a world that represented the inside of their 'creative

minds', visualising it via elements of their work. But Alex pitched back to them, suggesting, "Let's give the world its own identity and put these elements into it, so the artists' styles don't juxtapose too badly. If I can contain the world, then the two artists could exist inside it... so I might reinterpret references from what they do into an illustration." Alex sketched up the concepts for the worlds, and sold the idea to the client on this basis.

I love my Gut world incorporated the work of Interspectacular and Joshua Davis, bringing their imagery onto the Gut world in the form of a yeti, hotdogs fighting with sauce bottles and Davis's flowers and erupting volcano demonstrating vector drawing – each vignette being a visual analogy of a new tool being introduced to the Suite. The user is initially introduced to the worlds as they rotate around the screen, selecting the one to view. Elements on the worlds start moving, commencing the narratives. Clicking on various characters within the world, such as the yeti, activates a flow of events which then offer new choices for interaction. Some of these lead to videos of the artists talking about how they use the new Adobe tools in their work, while others offer short texts on the tools.

Once the project was approved a team was put together, with Alex directing and colleague Robert Bader overseeing interactive direction and concept ideas for all elements within the worlds. As it would have been too much for a single individual within the short production schedule, Alex directed a team of animators,

I love my Gut
Interactive promotional website for Adobe Creative Suite 2.3 software package.
Agency: Goodby, Silverstein & Partners, USA, 2006

illustrators and developers, with one animator handling the ever-present monkey character for consistency of character and personality, and others working more loosely across the three worlds, "I'd done some of the work," Alex explains, "but then I had to put the Art Director hat on and start making a commercial project. I would love to have done all the pieces, but it's part of the reality I have to face taking on roles like these."

Collaboration is a positive aspect of animation, although he acknowledges it can be hard to hand over the original ideas – "You've got to share" – and let others have fun with the piece too. "That's where the crossover really comes in: you hold the vision, but when you've got the team, because they're assigned a portion, they really think out their little scene. That's why with great animation it always feels like there's so much going on in there because someone's caring for that little bubble they have on the side, and they come back and a new idea is on the table. And it goes up a level. It's the best of both worlds." Alex cites an example of a dog that splits in two and sniffs its own backside, one of the amusing moments which recur throughout the site. These elements successfully combine within each world, with different colour palettes holding each world's various stories together.

Non-linear narratives were explored as a way to impart information and direct users around the site. For example, the monkey character covers the main functionality of moving between sections of the site and different worlds. Instead of using open, close, back or exit buttons, the monkey embodies the role of the 'guide', a familiar device in stories, films and games, which viewers can readily associate with. It was a playful way to make the world feel as alive as possible and maintain a narrative, rather than break it with harsher user-interface logic. "I felt this was an appropriate response because it was aimed at the

Creative Industry, who already deeply understood Adobe's suite of tools ... and after all it was meant to be the inside of a creative's mind, which I saw as a more intuitive, stream-of-consciousness kind of place."

Once the project was approved a team was put together, with Alex directing and colleague Robert Bader overseeing interactive direction and concept ideas for all elements within the worlds. Alex started with drawing to visualise his vision for the three worlds, but as it would have been too much for a single individual to cover all aspects within the short production schedule, he supervised a team of animators, illustrators and developers, "I would love to have done all the pieces, but it's part of the reality I have to face taking on roles like these." One animator handled the ever-present monkey character for consistency of character and personality, and others worked more loosely across the three worlds.

Freed from delivering an information-heavy launch, the lively site was a successful marketing tool, creating a lot of buzz for Adobe, with the monkey being utilised in the subsequent Creative Suite campaign, proving Alex's illustrative layered approach to be the right one.

The Creative Mind microsite can be seen at www.adobe.com/de/creativemind/microsite.html

Alex Jenkins lives in the UK.

(Above) **Impossible? Possible** (Right) **Must.Work.Fast**
Interactive website for Adobe Creative Suite, 2006

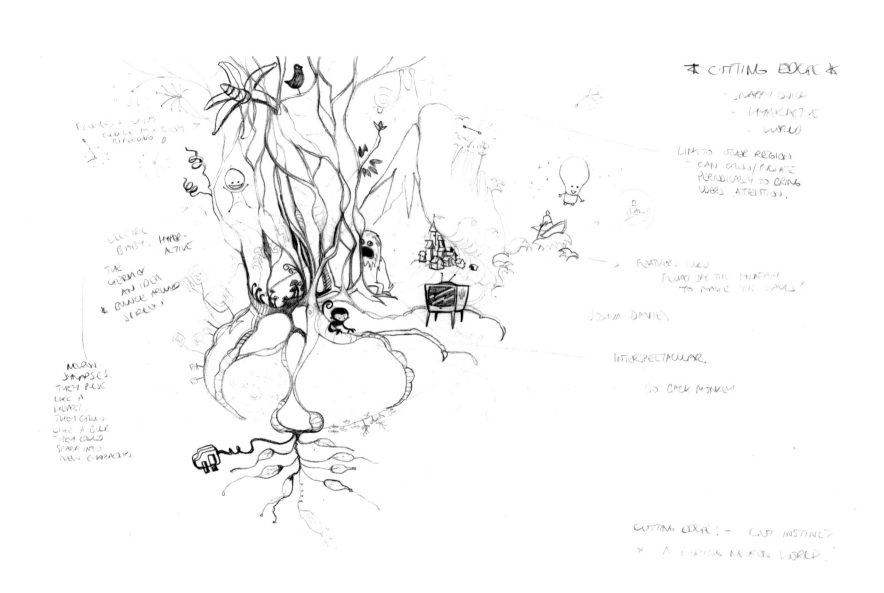

I love my Gut (sketch)
Interactive website for Adobe Creative Suite, 2006

Deliver Machine (above)
Deliver Bicycle Gears
Deliver HatTrick
Deliver Over the Wire
Mastheads for the website of *Deliver* magazine US Postal Service.
Agency: Cambel Ewald; art directors: Grayson Cardinell and Phil Foster,
2011 and 2012

Red Nose Studio
Deliver online magazine

Chris Sickels's intriguing vintage characters and Heath Robinson-like contraptions propelled from a bygone age into the hi-tech digital environment are a reminder of the magical capacity of illustration for creating unexpected realities. Three-dimensional illustration can add something distinctive to graphic contexts both on and off screen. This image is one of the solutions to a brief to create mastheads for the webpage of *Deliver*, the online magazine for the American postal service, the objective being to arrest the reader's attention, to draw them into the site. This is one of a set of four images to be used successively over the course of a year, all similar in format and function but autonomous in content.

This illustration "embodies what *Deliver* can facilitate in the relationship between marketers and consumers". In this case, *Deliver* is "the machine that utilises many aspects of communication to help the client reach their customers". Key words and phrases, such as *communication, information* and *moving from point A to point B*, were the catalyst for the concept, and Chris had a relatively free hand in developing the content for his images and in choosing which of his ideas to "construct". He reveals more about the function of the final illustration, showing that its use in a digital environment is fundamentally the same as when working in traditional formats. "It's about the message. Problem-solving and the visual ends combine. They go hand in hand." He acknowledges the allure of the thoughtfully lit, intriguing sets and their part in the communication process: "The eye-candy aspect is almost as important as the concept."

Mr H.B. Deux
Client: Society of Illustrators,
New York City. The Call for
Entries poster for *The 55th
Illustration Annual*, 2012.
Creative Director: John Hendrix

Youth
Personal work exploring the
possibilities of integrating
drawing with 3D work, 2012

Because the images Chris creates are convincing in their detail they create the impression of being snapshots of a magic reality, documenting part of an eccentric and often anachronistic world that extends beyond the frame. "I convey a core narrative and allow the single frame to have a life before and after. That's what the viewer brings to the table." The potential to be animated, especially in this screen-based context, is obvious. Although he has made work for films Chris makes salient points that have relevance to ongoing debates pertaining to the impact of the ubiquitous opportunities to add motion to imagery. Notably, one may ask whether motion would extend the context of the work or if that would be merely "trickery or eye candy". "I believe that in a poignant and efficient way a still image can say a lot. The power of illustration refines a concept; it doesn't have to describe the text. It allows the viewer to read between the lines."

This acknowledgement of the viewer as an active player in the communication process reflects Chris's sense of how his own work functions. "I get excited when people get drawn in." He clarifies that, "it's doing what it's supposed to do when people react to it." Although he engineers the narrative as the vehicle for the metaphor, he also reveals, "I'm not a storyteller per se – there's a skill to that. There's not a specific story directly within the image. I like to give the viewer more to pull from it."

Holistic Visualization (simplifying complex data)
Computer World, 2011. Art Director: April Montgomery

Each commission provides an opportunity for Chris to invent new characters in an ever-expanding cast that, "are fantasy – they do things I couldn't do". He invests them with particular power and they perform an important function within the illustrative process. "My work is less conceptual and more character-based – I give the characters personalities: I force them to be physically active. They need to carry the message through their expressions, gesture and positions."

Chris is a fastidious and skilful craftsman attentive to the physical properties of the materials he selects, their individual "patina". He often chooses to construct with recycled elements because of their inherent qualities, the textures that, "say so much", that add layers and bring both tactility and authenticity to a piece. Irrespective of the seductive aesthetic of the puppets and props, he is nevertheless emphatic that the primary objective is to make a piece of visual communication through the illusion of an imagined reality, not an object with an independent life. "I build through the camera's eye and the 2D element is at the forefront – the sculpture isn't the end product." Although the puppets are enduring, the world they inhabit is ephemeral, "the model has a texture. You can hold it in your hand but they are created to be seen from one angle in an environment that doesn't exist, a diorama that will be put away and maybe used again. After the photo that world is gone – it's a piece of illustration." Illustration representing a synthesis of digital and traditional worlds.

Chris Sickels is the illustrator behind Red Nose Studio and lives and works in the USA.

Stilty
Personal work – the artist explores the possibilities of integrating drawing with his 3D work

Wake Up Call
Client: Planadviser, 2012.
Art Director: Soojin Buzelli

"To be able to let your drawings move with music and sound is something very magical – when senses combine to create something greater than their separate parts."

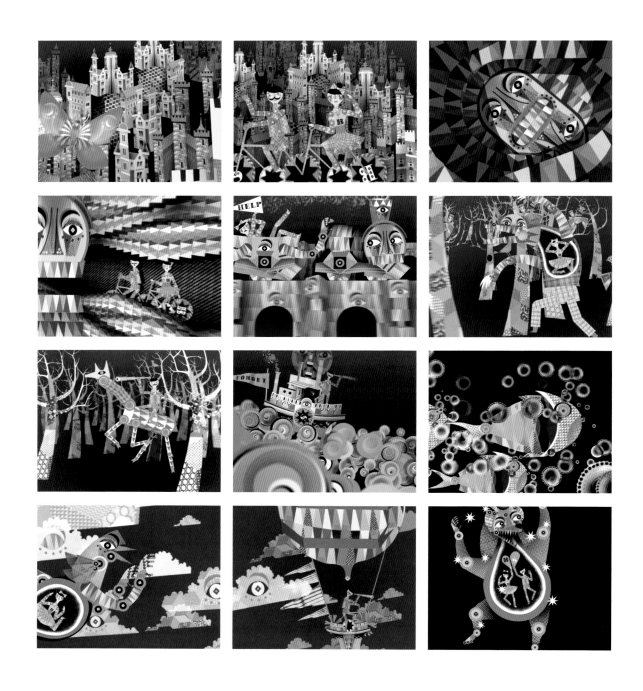

Stills from video for **I Didn't See It Coming** (Richard X version) by Belle and Sebastian.
Animation and production by Lesley Barnes, taken from the *Come on Sister* 12 inch, Rough Trade Records, 2011

Lesley Barnes
I Didn't See It Coming video

Music videos are an essential tool for the promotion of singles, and they need to be distinctive to catch the attention of potential music buyers. In spite of often limited budgets, animated videos have often proved to be very successful in achieving this, and animator/illustrator Lesley Barnes has brought a special quality to I Didn't See It Coming for Scottish band Belle and Sebastian. The film follows a happy, paper-cut-style couple through town, forest and seascapes as their journey darkens and perils are faced, with patterns and textures effectively employed to enhance the visual storytelling.

Starting out as an animator, Lesley expanded her skills into illustration, and much of her work is heavily influenced by folk art. "I love the way that stories and meanings are woven into the patterns and imagery," she says, and her intention with this animation was to capture this sort of narrative for the video's visuals so that an extra layer of meaning was created around the song's music and lyrics. "I was also influenced by vintage children's book illustration," she adds, "which felt appropriate, as Belle and Sebastian were named after a French children's book series about a girl and her dog."

Following the creation of a T-shirt and tote-bag design for the band, they gave Lesley free creative reign, liaising with band member Sarah Martin over preparatory drawings, character puppets and snippets of animation for the video. "She seemed happy to let me do my own thing – which is very unusual – and indulge my dancing-bear obsession. I think not being given a brief can be daunting, though, as constraints can give you something to grab hold of initially." Although the video was mostly created digitally, all the characters started life as paper puppets, and the intention was to retain a feeling of the handmade throughout the film.

Belle and Sebastian have a loyal following, and although Lesley believes the audience should always be taken into consideration when creating an artwork or animation, she feels it is also important for an artist to stay true to their own style and vision. "So although I obviously didn't want to alienate any Belle and Sebastian fans, I also wanted to tell the story that I felt when I heard the music for the first time."

Lesley listened to I Didn't See It Coming many times, "sometimes just to hear the words, and sometimes just the music," with the song's music dictating the tempo

Promotional images for
I Didn't See It Coming
By Belle and Sebastian, 2011

of the animation and suggesting where scenes should change or events should take place. The lyrics, on the other hand, dictated more of the narrative and the imagery. "For this song I pictured B and S, a boy and girl happy and in love, but with a kind of sword of Damocles hanging over this contentment – the events they 'didn't see coming'. I also felt that the music and lyrics had the sense of a journey like a train/bike ride, so I presented the narrative as a trip through a magical land via different modes of transport – bikes, trains, ships and an airship."

Wanting to create a complete world across the animation so that the viewer felt immersed in both the music and the visuals, Lesley started with these two main characters, B and S, and built up the other creature and scenic elements around them. "I love stage sets, so I approached the whole animation with that kind of flat, also three-dimensional, perspective in mind. The characters were all created like paper puppets and I wanted both the movement and the style of the whole animation to capture this papery world." Circles feature throughout the artwork, an extension of the first image that came to Lesley when she initially heard the song – "an unstoppable wheel spinning and spinning".

Having previously worked on her animations alone, Lesley put together a small team comprising herself, Matt Saunders and Bruce Cameron to work on *I Didn't See It Coming*. Her collaborators brought their own touches to the video: Matt's main job was creating the spinning sea scene, while Bruce was responsible for bringing many of the animal characters to life.

Animation, for Lesley, is an inimitable pleasure that creates a unique product. "To be able to let your drawings move with music and sound is something very magical – when senses combine to create something greater than their separate parts."

I Didn't See It Coming can be seen at http://vimeo.com/23793374

Lesley Barnes lives in Scotland, UK.

Rug
Designed for Node, a non-profit social business.
Handmade by a fair trade group of traditional Nepalese carpet makers, 2013

Sleeping Beauty
Artwork for exhibition celebrating the
200th anniversary of The Grimm Brothers'
Fairy Tales, 2012

The Illustrators

Victor Ambrus 80
www.victorambrus.com

Gail Armstrong 36
www.illustrationweb.com/artists/GailArmstrong

Lesley Barnes 166
www.lesleybarnes.co.uk

Serge Bloch 116
www.sergebloch.net

Steve Brodner 94
www.stevebrodner.com

George Butler 54
www.georgebutler.org

Jill Calder 134
www.jillcalder.com

Christopher Corr 72
www.christophercorr.com

Sara Fanelli 26
www.sarafanelli.com

Craig Foster 76
www.illustrationweb.com/artists/CraigFoster
www.fostermed.com
www.medillsb.com/ArtistPortfolioThumbs.aspx?AID=282

Edu Fuentes 112
www.edufuentes.com

Peter Grundy 84
www.grundini.com

George Hardie 40
www.archive.agda.com.au/eventsnews/national/events/2006/George.html
www.artworkersguild.org/member/georgehardie

Asaf Hanuka 18
www.asafhanuka.com

Tomer Hanuka 18
www.thanuka.com

Emma Houlston 138
www.penandthepixel.com

Anne Howeson 58
www.annehoweson.com

Barbara Hulanicki 148
www.barbarahulanickidesign.com

Richard Johnson 50
www.newsillustrator.com
www.internationalsocietyofwarartists.blogspot.com
www.news.nationalpost.com/2011/03/10/wounded-warriors-2

The Authors

Authors of *Making Great Illustration* (A&C Black, 2011), on illustrators' processes and *Becoming A Successful Illustrator* (Fairchild Books, 2013) **Derek Brazell** and **Jo Davies**, have been collaborating since the late 1990's, when as board members of the Association of Illustrators keen to create a platform for discussion and investigation into the subject of illustration they developed *the journal* which they edited until their subsequent launch of internationally acclaimed *Varoom* magazine in 2006. Through expansion of writing on the subject they believe that illustration will continue to be increasingly recognised for its widespread cultural contribution.

Jo Davies

As an illustrator Jo has worked since the 1980s for major clients across advertising and design as well as for publishers. She is a published children's author who has exhibited her artwork internationally in the USA and Europe and been a speaker on invited panels at the Bologna Children's Book Fair.

In addition to receiving awards from Korea and Italy she has many times been included in *Images – The Best of British Illustration* – and in 2012 was a merit award winner for the prestigious 3x3 illustration awards in the USA. Her ongoing interest and practice in drawing involved her in a major research project, culminating in the publication of the book *Drawing – The Process* (Intellect, 2005) which she co-edited, alongside the curation of a major touring exhibition.

Jo devised the academic research network *VaroomLab* which has brought together universities and individuals from the academic community as a unique international network. She is editor in chief of *VaroomLabJournal*.

Her career as writer and illustrator has been combined with work in education at all levels, and she has also represented illustration nationally through the Higher Education Academy. She holds the post of Associate Professor in Illustration at Plymouth University.

Derek Brazell

As a practitioner, writer and advisor, Derek has been involved in the illustration world for many years. He is known for several successful children's books, including *Cleversticks* for Harper Collins, in print since 1992, and *Lima's Red Hot Chilli*, another long-term success, for Mantra. His illustrations have been included in many exhibitions, including *Images – The Best of British Illustration*.

He delivers lectures on careers and ethical issues in illustration for universities and at illustration events including *Pick Me Up* and *Artsmart*, and has been closely involved in the international VaroomLab peer review network through his role as *Varoom* magazine publisher at the Association of Illustrators.

Derek has closely supported illustrators in all areas of their careers, has spoken on illustrators' rights at the Bologna Children's Book Fair and campaigned for creators rights through his work with the Pro-Action visual artists' group and the European Illustrators' Forum. He was a member of the Creators' Council of the Design and Artists Copyright Society for its five-year duration and was Director for Visual Arts on the British Copyright Council Board for three years.

Fine Illustration
Self generated, 2012

Peppermint Tea
Self generated, 2013

Other books by **Derek Brazell** and **Jo Davies**

Making Great Illustration
Published by A&C Black, 2011

Making Great Illustration examines the work of some of the world's best illustrators, with images of their artwork, portraits and photos of their studios, revealing the generally hidden processes involved in the creation of illustration from concept to finished work. The book was written from face-to-face interviews and covers a wide range of illustrative practice looking at both the conceptual and practical approaches of this huge variety of international artists.
ISBN 978-1-408-12453-6

'Beautifully curated ... One of the loveliest aspects of the book is the attention to detail throughout. The photography is excellent, giving a real sense of each artist's workspace ... Making Great Illustration reveals the 21st century illustration world to be in rather rude health.'
Steve Pill, Artists & Illustrators magazine

'A rich array of important, exciting and inspirational work, intelligently collated.'
Kirsten Hardie, The Arts University College at Bournemouth

Becoming A Successful Illustrator
Published by Fairchild Books/Bloomsbury, 2013

An essential guide for new illustrators and graduates covering areas to work in; the professional world of the illustrator; self promotion; getting your work seen; finance and running a business and more. With newly commissioned artworks and insightful comments from international illustrators accompanied by examples of their work supporting the text.
ISBN 9782940411931

'A great class reference for students entering their junior and senior years.'
Alaiyo Bradshaw, Parsons The New School for Design, USA

'...highly useful and relevant to both national and international audiences.'
Chris Draper, Cambridge School of Art, UK